A mother shares her journey of her daughter's recovery from Autism and Sensory Processing Disorder to Functioning Recovery and independent living while providing helpful tips for other parents.

TAMI A. GOLDSTEIN

FOREWORD WRITTEN BY SUSAN VAUGHAN KRATZ, OTR, CST

DENVER, COLORADO

NOTE: A portion of the profits will be donated to the SPD Foundation. (The Sensory Processing Disorder Foundation expands knowledge, fosters awareness and promotes recognition of Sensory Processing Disorders.)

Contents

Introduction

I AM WRITING this book from my perspective; not my husband's, my son's or even Heather's, though this is her story. My husband supported us financially and accepted that I would seek interventions and supports even if I couldn't quite explain why or how they would help. As a mom, I knew that this was important and that time was essential. I didn't know how this was going to happen but intuitively, as a mom, I knew how important my efforts would be for Heather's future and, of course, I was willing to do anything and everything in my power to help my child in need.

My son was a child struggling to grow up with the focus being on his sister too much of the time. I am grateful to say he has always watched out for her and they have a close relationship today. My son is 4 ½ years older than Heather. He was a strong fighter and had qualities, even at a young age, which left no doubt he could make his way in the world. Heather did not. When the doctors used the words **life-threatening**, I couldn't stop until I did everything in my power to help my child in need. It's a conflict any good mom would have; you want to give 110% to each child you have.

The intention of this book is to encourage networking between moms with children on the Autism Spectrum. Networking helped me to help Heather achieve Functioning Recovery; it was a step along the journey.

This is Tip #1. Call your friends and ask if they know anyone who has a child on the Autism Spectrum. *(Refer to Appendix A for all Tips).*

Get their name and number and call them. We, moms, understand. We speak each other's language and we like to speak. That unique language may lead you down a path that provides help; a clue to guide you. It was networking with other moms that lead me to try interventions. I was told by some to "stop looking for something" to help Heather. I may not have otherwise taken this path if it wasn't for the networking mothers. We have had frequent discussions about how all of us, moms with children with Autism, have a different story but yet it's the same story because we have the same struggle.

I see people with Asperger's as a beautiful bright thread in the rich tapestry of life.

– Tony Attwood

Foreword

IT IS WITH great pleasure that I write the forward for this book. To every parent who expresses gratitude over the improvements and positive changes their child has made due to their experiences at our clinic, I always challenge them to "write a book and tell your story". Personal stories are evident truths. Personal stories are as important as scientific research. Personal stories have the power to 'prove the effectiveness' of clinical interventions.

Over the years I have witnessed the evolution of families becoming empowered with information as they struggle to understand, cope with, and help their children's issues. This explosion of access to information has helped increase public awareness of the problems associated with sensory processing disorders and neurological instability. People communicate daily through blogs and chat rooms online. Parents attend support groups in virtual meeting rooms. There is now a magazine dedicated to disseminating helpful information to parents with children with sensory processing issues. A clinic in Denver is solely dedicated to researching and guiding both professionals and parents through the convoluted journey that is sensory processing dysfunction. There are extremely dedicated scientists and therapists working at obtaining a diagnostic code for medical insurance reimbursement. The more 'individual stories' that are told not only affirm these people's work, but also bring hope and power to those families who are not finding answers for their children's daily struggles in functioning and coping.

Sensory Integration is a natural neurological phenomenon. When it is dysfunctional it is often a hidden problem. It is often misunderstood as behavioral problems. If a child cannot verbally tell their parent that the fabric of all clothing feels bad, then the adult has to interpret that child's behavior. But if that same child could tell us that by moving around quickly prevents the clothes from touching skin, we might have an easier understanding of what is often called hyperactivity. The sensory environment of many public buildings, like a school, is frequently overloaded with an abundance of sensory stimuli. A person with a typical nervous system usually can turn off the buzz and the flicker of fluorescent lighting; the odors from cleaning products; the presence of too many in one's personal space; the acoustic assault from a loud PA system or the noise within the cafeteria. For those who can't screen out these sensations such environments can force a person to cope beyond their abilities. Furthermore, if sensations such as touch and body sense are not registering into awareness, the person cannot make subtle and discreet adjustments to motor skills. These kids are frequently misunderstood and met with differing expectations from others.

Sensory Processing Disorder affects a large number of children and adults, yet continues to go under-diagnosed and commonly poses a challenge to professionals who haven't been educated about this perspective. Characteristics common to Sensory Processing Disorder are similar to other disorders or are concurrent with other labels, including but not limited to: ADHD; Autism; Asperger's; Learning Disabled; Dyslexia; Hyperlexia; Clumsiness; Mood Disorder; and Anxiety.

Sensory Integration, or Sensory Processing, involves the ability to register and organize sensory information for use. This ability to accurately sense, interpret and organize a variety of simultaneous inputs allows the individual to adapt to and respond adequately to environmental demands. Our perceptual system is constructed so that what we experience feels like physical reality. Making a purposeful response to our perceptions of touch, movement (vestibular), body sense (proprioception), vision, hearing, taste, and smell is how we master the world. How we occupy our time is one measure of how we adaptively respond to sensations. The profession of Occupational Therapy is rooted in facilitating an individual's engagement in purposeful activity, or "occupations". These activities include everything a person has to accomplish or do from the time they wake up in the morning to the quality of their sleep the next night. Few professions study the theory of sensory integration from an occupational viewpoint. The originator of this theory, A. Jean Ayres, was both an occupational therapist and a research scientist.

For decades occupational therapists who specialize in the advanced practice of Sensory Integration methods have endured criticism over the lack of empirical evidence for diagnosis and treatment. What compounds the problem is we can't yet visualize or document the neuro-plastic changes in the brain that occur in response to treatment. We have to rely on behavior to make direct or indirect correlations on how someone's senses are integrating.

One challenge is that behavioral observations are open to many different interpretations. Different philosophies guide various professional groups, influencing the linguistically defined terminology they each use to interpret behavior. For example, when a child has feeding issues a psychologist may interpret this as anxiety, but an occupational therapist may notice hyper-responsiveness to touch, taste, and smell. The bottom line is the child hates eating food and mealtime is consistently a struggle for the family. The semantics of descriptions can often lead families away from finding the right help for their child.

As a therapist, I am charged with utilizing all my clinical knowledge and tools at my disposal, using critical reasoning skills as the best plan of action. When a parent brings their child to meet me, they are saying, "I don't understand why my smart child can't make it and I want your help." For children with behavioral challenges, the long standing trend of prescribing medication to 'see how it goes' is being recognized as merely a means of masking symptoms. However, the quality of life and the nature of sensory processing dysfunction can be overwhelming and all encompassing. Some children and their families are living in survival mode until they can find help.

Empathy is a crucial skill to possess in order to be able to help people with sensory processing dysfunction. To empathize means to share, to experience the feelings of another person. It also reflects the ability to put oneself into the mental shoes of another person to understand her emotions and feelings. Over the years I have come to understand that my childhood was effected by auditory hypersensitivity. My emotional and interpersonal development was shaped around my short fuse when the sounds in my world 'assaulted' my ears. Not until I sought treatment (as an adult therapist learning treatment strategies) did I understand this. Once my brain changed with various therapies I tried myself, I became aware of a difference of calmness deep inside. I don't think I had ever felt that before. So did my own sensory processing issues make me a good candidate as a therapist to work with this issue? Was I born with this empathy skill? Probably yes.

My clients and their families have helped me understand that behavior is a nonverbal way for a child to communicate who they are and what they need. I have also come to learn that behavior and emotions can be effected by either unidentified illness or chronic pain. Though sensory integration is not identified as an illness, an increasing amount of evidence is linking biological markers as subclinical problems. Examples: heavy metal toxicity, vaccine injuries, food and metabolic difficulties, gut and brain connections, and lack of essential elements necessary for life's building blocks may be missing in our food. It is not the purpose of this story to elaborate on this point. I only make this point that evolving evidence suggests biological markers should be considered when families are searching for help.

Over my 30 years as a clinician, I have come to place value and faith in clinical outcomes from our clients, and from published case studies. I rely on empirically designed scientific studies to support and affirm various diagnostic and therapeutic modalities we try in the clinic. It is very hard to dispute the truth of a person's story, especially when the outcomes can be compared to all the other things a family has tried to address their child's problems. Families can't wait for definitive research before they seek help. It is common for families as a unit to be stressed over their child's situation. Lack of resources or financial strains can also compound the problems.

If a child can't tell what's going on inside, the next best thing is to hear the parent's version of the story. The best second act to such a story is for the child to grow up and tell their personal reality. Thank you, Tami, for writing this book. Each small truth can collectively help change the world.

Susan Vaughan Kratz, OTR, CST

Dedication

TO HEATHER, WHO changed the way I see the world, opened my eyes to embrace new things and in the process made me a better person. I love my beautiful sweet girl!

To my husband, Stan, the love of my life, who never stopped loving me even when he didn't understand me.

To my 2 BFF's, Betsy and Honey, who stood up for me at my wedding 33 years ago, stayed close throughout my18 moves to 5 states. You offered endless advice, were great sounding boards, offered research help, gave educational tips and "slapped me upside the head" to keep me focused. You are my sisters.

To my mom, who saw in Heather what I saw and guided me with her love.

Biography

THIS JOURNEY BEGINS with a mother's love for her daughter. After learning her daughter was on the Autism Spectrum, Tami began to tirelessly educate herself in the sciences of: Behavioral Health, Child Psychology, Human Anatomy, Occupational Health, Pharmacology, Therapeutic Massage and Bodywork and has been a parent advocate for her daughter since 1997.

In 2002, as her knowledge and passion grew, Tami began reaching out to other families in need of help. In 2005, Tami founded the Rock County Autism Support Group and she is the community resource liaison for the SPD (Sensory Processing Disorders) Parent Connections Support Group of Rock County and the surrounding areas. Since 2005, Tami has been State and Nationally Certified in Therapeutic Massage and Bodywork. She continued her training and in 2013 completed her certification requirements needed in CranioSacral Therapy with the Upledger Institute in Florida.

Tami currently has two offices where she facilitates CranioSacral Therapy. Approximately 38% of her clientele are children, teenagers and young adults on the Autism Spectrum or with other neuro-developmental delays. When asked to lecture, Tami uses her personal experience, extensive knowledge, and dedication to help others learn about and understand the medical and educational aspects of Autism, Autism Spectrum Disorders and SPD.

Acknowledgements

TO CHERYL "SMITTY Phair" Smith for your inspirations, talented typing skills, sharp editing eyes, and for the thirty plus years of dedication to teaching in public education. You are my Irish Sister!! Thank you and Slainte!

[Smitty, a Music Teacher for thirty-three years, just finished writing an e-book entitled, <u>Lights, Camera, Kids!</u> Successful Ideas to Inspire Your Creative Productions. Go to <u>www.Cheryl-Smitty-Smith.com</u> for the ebook and also a newly recorded children's CD, <u>The Apple Twistin' Song</u>.]

I also want to acknowledge Heather Goldstein, Brenda Mathews and Jenny Mathews, for ideas for the cover photo and the author's picture.

I want to acknowledge Jill Fogerty of Flutterbye Photography for Heather's photo.

CHAPTER 1

ADHD, OCD, SPD, ASD
Alphabet Soup…or Is This a Diagnosis?

Genius is eternal patience

– Michaelangelo

Doctors and Their Diagnoses

THIS IS THE story about Heather, our daughter, and our journey to help her get to where she is today. Imagine hearing a diagnosis of your young child: ADD (Attention Deficit Disorder), ADHD (Attention Deficit Hyperactive Disorder), OCD (Obsessive Compulsive Disorder), and ODD (Obsessive Defiant Disorder). I wasn't sure if we were making alphabet soup or if this was a diagnosis.

I remember Heather as a baby; feed me, change me, and put me down. She didn't like to be cuddled or swaddled. When I held my skin to her skin for too long, she would get a rash and she also hated to feel stickiness.

She really didn't play with other children. She played next to them. She seemed to be in her own world and it was always her own make-believe world. She told me about her imaginary friends. These stories were very focused and detailed. It was difficult to distract her away from that world and back into reality. She would get physically upset with me if I didn't set a place at the table for her friend(s). I also noticed slight tremors as if she was chilled and bumping into things. If she was naughty, I would put her into time-out for the number of minutes which corresponded to her age. When her time was up, she would stay there. I would encourage her to leave her time-out area whenever she was ready but she would just sit in her chair and stare at the wall for what felt like an eternity.

My family is from the East Coast and I would often go to the seashore with my friends. After getting blankets and lounge chairs arranged, these mothers ran up and down the beach chasing their toddlers. Heather never left the perimeter of any-sized comforter we laid down. She was so adverse to the feel of sand. She wouldn't touch it with her finger or hand and she certainly wouldn't walk on it. If you lifted her up to put her in the sand, she'd contort her body so she wouldn't have to touch it. She felt the same way about grass. She would rather wear her socks in the grass than be barefooted. When she crawled, it was more of a crab-crawl. She didn't want her knees to touch the ground. Labels and seams in her clothing caused irritations. There were so many sensitivities. We laughed about it back then. We thought that this was just the way that Heather was. Parents accept their children the way they are because they are your kids and you love them.

We moved to Maryland when Heather was approximately four years old. I spoke to her pediatrician and a child psychologist whom he recommended in order to seek more answers. We tried to fulfill the suggestions from this doctor to help with Heather's sensitivities. We changed the soaps that we used; we bought all natural cottons, etc. He also felt that her focus was too narrow and he recommended that we should broaden her horizons. We felt that ballet classes would be the perfect match for her slow and methodical ways and also improve her continual clumsiness and awkward movements since she responded so well to music. Every child responds so differently. My son was like the television show, The Electric Company. We'd open the door to leave; it was go-go-go, boisterous, fun, and we just went-went-went. Heather would meander to the door. She was more like the show, Mr. Rogers. She lived in a quiet neighborhood. She might open that door and look out but she'd step back and close it. It wasn't every day that she wanted to go outside. Heather was involved in the ballet class but for her it was organized play. At five and six years old, her make-believe world and non-interaction with other children surfaced continually.

As children get older, they learn new things. We couldn't get Heather to that next step. She wasn't evolving. It was a struggle to get her up and moving. In some situations, it didn't matter what we did or how we tried to comfort her, it was a losing battle. We were not able to calm her down.

As she got older, her behaviors became worse in certain environments. With some teachers' environments in school, she would not only pass but she would excel. With other teachers, she would literally shut down. Educationally, this continued to be a problem with each school year. She also disappeared from environments. She didn't want people in the house. When we had people visiting for a holiday, I had to beg Heather to come out of her room long enough to eat the meal. She hibernated in her bedroom. As a young child, she slept but as a teenager, she slept for days. We watched Heather's maladaptive behaviors escalate and her health deteriorate substantially between Fourth Grade and Eighth Grade. These behaviors drove me to find more answers. Each time I would learn something new, I researched it online. I was doing these investigations in 1999 when most homes didn't have computers. I felt very fortunate to explore these new topics in the comfort of my home. New answers would bring new questions to mind. For example: Why could Heather have such unbelievable focus on certain things and not on others? Why could she learn entire dialogues and passages from movies and musicals but yet she was

ADD/ADHD? Where did the hyper-activity fit in when my child was the one sound asleep in the middle of chaos? Why was Heather diagnosed with OCD when she exhibited none of the symptoms? Being diagnosed with so many different labels, how did one affect the other? These types of questions led me to ask more and more questions.

As Heather was getting older, it was getting more difficult to motivate her. We couldn't get her up in the morning. She slept like the dead. We couldn't drag her out of bed. Behavior charts, earning stars, or any method of motivation didn't work. If I set an alarm and it jarred her awake, the situation would escalate. I noticed how I could intensify the situation if I raised my voice. Heather shut down and then cried, thinking that I didn't love her. These patterns resulted in her continuously being late for school.

When we received this massive ADD, ADHD, OCD, ODD diagnosis, we were overwhelmed with the variety of pharmaceuticals that the doctors recommended. We certainly didn't want to use **every** medication for each of the different labels. We didn't know where to go. I kept seeking answers and asking more and more questions. When I didn't like the answers, I continued to ask more questions. As Heather grew and changed, there was a need to ask additional questions.

My husband was in a field of work which offered many promotions. Each of these advancements resulted in a move to a different area and each move required a different pediatrician or child psychologist to look at our situation. Before Heather entered Second Grade, my husband was again transferred and we moved to the state of Wisconsin. It was during this school year that I began to notice some educational differences. She couldn't read English. We are Jewish and Heather attended Sunday school where she could read Hebrew at a Fourth Grade level. Most people would assume that it would be more difficult to learn a foreign language, especially one which read from right to left, but Heather excelled. It was the English language that she couldn't read. Why was there a difference? Why would she have an easier time with one than the other? This really concerned me and I began to ask even more questions.

As the years advanced, the gap widened with differences between the students who were her age. Sometimes when she spoke, the words were not in sequential order. It was difficult to understand what she was trying to communicate. She had a difficult time getting to the facts. The more excited she was, the more difficult it was to understand her exceedingly detailed story. Also, there was something that wasn't right with the way Heather went to sleep. She would pass out; she would get to a point where she couldn't be awakened. It was a complete shut-down.

In Fourth Grade, she started to seek small confined places. Our first pediatrician, (Pediatrician "A") referred us to a child psychologist. It was 1996; we got the second diagnosis of ADD. This child psychologist discussed Heather's intellect, her school's need to be prepared to accommodate her, especially in Math, and eventual advanced placement for Reading and Language. He talked about her strengths in Music and how it could be used to enrich her auditory processing skills. He talked about the need for visual input. He had a concern though; he wrote; "One thing to be kept in mind is Heather's stress producing surgical history. Emerging clinical data suggest that stress producing life events in childhood have a develop-mental impact on neuro-transmitter receptors in the brain. This means that sensory input may need to be stronger in one or more of the sensory input areas. Heather can be taught to be quickly aware of stress reactions in her body and the subsequent application of stress management exercises which will moderate the autonomic arousal which most likely will affect the processing of new information in challenging situations." We brought this information to her school psychologist to implement some supports. [In reference to part of the doctor's quote: "stress-producing surgical history": Between the ages of five and twelve, Heather had a medical condition that required a number of surgical procedures which resolved this issue.]

Sixth grade brought further decline and rigidity in needs for Heather. It also brought about insurance changes. Heather was deteriorating so we welcomed the change to go to Pediatrician "B" in Medical Facility "B". He was an ADD/ADHD Specialist and he evaluated Heather as having ADHD. He then referred her to a therapist and suggested some medication changes for the behaviors. Our new insurance was such that we weren't able to visit the therapist which he had recommended. Instead, we went to a doctor which the insurance provider allowed. She was a wonderful social worker in Whitewater, WI. We saw her for quite some time. At this point, I was taking Heather to her appointments as she was kicking and screaming. If I said that the sky was blue, she would argue that it wasn't. It didn't matter what I said, everything was a fight. This wasn't the way that I wanted to have a relationship with my child. It was very demanding to work full time, have another child and a husband, and deal with Heather's behaviors but we were in crisis and something had to be done. I explained to Heather that I was the parent and I was responsible, until she was eighteen years old, for her health and well-being. I also told her that I didn't care if she talked or didn't talk during the weekly appointments but we were going to go. We went every week and I talked about how things were at home. Heather had gone from approximately ninety pounds in Sixth Grade to sixty pounds in Eighth Grade. She was eating so this wasn't the issue. She was finicky about what she ate but she still ate. She was dropping weight at a rapid rate. During this time, she had many rashes. A blister would put her down for days.

As Heather got older, there were days where she couldn't function. After being picked up from school, she would literally crawl from the car to her bedroom and into her closet. Once there, she would rock back and forth and flap her hands in the air. As a parent, this was the scariest thing I'd ever seen. I felt that she was on the brink of losing her mind. This was not right. We were baffled as to what to do. We were seeking answers but not getting the information we needed.

After a time, our social worker, having labeled Heather OCD and ODD, referred us to a child psychologist. I will never forget the day that this doctor said that he felt Heather's condition was more than her current diagnosis. He thought that she had Asperger's Syndrome. We had never heard of this. He took out a book with all types of diagnoses which he allowed us to read and study. Afterwards, I thought that this doctor might really be onto something. He explained that Asperger's was High-Functioning Autism. This was a new diagnosis for us and we needed to figure out what to do from this point.

> Imagine driving a car that isn't working well. When you step on the gas, the car sometimes lurches forward and sometimes doesn't respond. When you blow the horn it sounds blaring. The brakes sometimes slow the car down but not always. The blinkers work occasionally, the steering is erratic and the speedometer is inaccurate. You are engaged in a constant struggle to keep the car on the road and it's difficult to concentrate on anything else.
>
> – Dr. Stanley Greenspan

CHAPTER 2

Asperger's Syndrome Is High-Functioning Autism
Growing Up Heather

You cannot open a book without learning something

– *Confucius*

What Is Asperger's? And That's Heather? How?

I KNEW NOTHING about Asperger's Syndrome! My online research revealed; this condition was originally named for Hans Asperger in 1944; he studied children some of whom lacked non-verbal communication skills; had limited empathy with their peers; were physically clumsy; had eccentric or repetitious behaviors; could be preoccupied with rituals; had a limited range of interest; and could be skilled or exceptionally talented in Math or Music. Further research showed that Asperger's is a High-Functioning Autism which affects boys four out of five times over girls; people with Asperger's could have normal intelligence and near-normal language development but they may develop problems communicating as they get older. I also learned that girls' characteristics are different; their focus is not as narrow, they tend to have more eating issues, and are more prone to self-abuse than overt melt-downs directed at others. There is a continuum for Autism, Autistic Spectrum Disorders. Classic Autism is the lowest functioning level then Pervasive Developmental Disorder followed by Asperger's then ADD, and ADHD. All have the same characteristics but in various degrees.

How did my child get to be twelve years old without anyone realizing that she had Autism? Is Asperger's Syndrome High-Functioning Autism or is this just "growing up Heather"? I had two different aspects going on and I didn't really know if they were related to each other or not. I did know that day to day, I was fighting to work, trying to make everyone happy, trying to keep it together, and trying to motivate Heather. Her behaviors kept getting odder. Almost in Sixth Grade, her tic was out of control. What was once a childhood shutter was now a hand-wringing, shoulder-elevated, head-cocked-to-one-side (with head, neck, and shoulder tremors) behavior that would last from a few seconds up to a minute. A recent evaluation explained it as an Involuntary Habit. What's an Involuntary Habit? It was like an oxymoron to me. The choices were: if the tic becomes uncontrollable, they would medicate or ultimately perform exploratory brain surgery. After a seventy-two hour brain study, they noticed that Heather was having approximately forty of these tics per day but it wasn't in the area of the brain that they considered Epilepsy. In neurological studies, they discovered that she had no R.E.M. (Rapid Eye Movement) cycle in her sleep stages. The R.E.M. cycle rests and rejuvenates the body. She wasn't getting good, quality sleep therefore she was constantly exhausted.

At this point, I was dealing with Heather's medications and mental health aspects. What was I going to do? I didn't want to put her on more medications. I watched her deteriorate from weight-loss. She declined from about ninety pounds in Sixth Grade to about sixty-five pounds in Eighth Grade. Even though she would only eat certain foods, prepared the same way day after day, she ate like there was no tomorrow. I wasn't sure what to do. The scariest thing, for me, at that point was watching the drastic changes in

Heather's appearance before and after school. She left for school as a focused, bright-eyed-bushy-tailed student and returned as a totally different person. It was a level of fatigue which was beyond normal. I watched her exit the school. As she got closer to the car, she started to break down. Her shoulders would begin to slump and her head would droop. She would almost curl up as she got into our car and she didn't want to be touched. I learned to not even pat her on the back. She closed into herself not wanting to look at me or talk to me but I continued to ask her questions about her day with little or no response.

Typically, kids in Third and Fourth Grade are usually leaving the house after school to play with friends. Heather was not doing that. If anything, she was showing greater signs of deterioration. She took five-hour naps after school and we were still not able to wake her. If I tried to keep her awake until after dinner, she would fall asleep in her food at the table. Her depleted, passed-out state lasted for days. During the time Heather was awake, she would either ignore me or rage at me about everything. As parents, we tried every behavior modification tactic available to us. Nothing worked. I was so frustrated in the mornings, I told her: "You don't have to talk to me but you do have to get up, you have to get dressed, and you have to eat. You don't have to talk, you don't have to be nice but you do have to do these things." I tried everything to motivate her but things got worse.

After school in Sixth and Seventh Grade, instead of walking to the house, she would almost crawl where she headed for a small cubby-hole area in her closet. Once there, she would rock back and forth, shake and tremble, and cry. This would last for hours. We didn't know what to do. Once, we couldn't find her in the house. We eventually found her sound asleep in a bathroom cabinet. We made repeated visits to Pediatrician "B" continuing to ask for help. He referred us to a neuro-psychologist who, after her evaluation, diagnosed Heather with anxiety, not-otherwise-specified (NOS). I had another answer but still had more questions because of Heather's deterioration. No one was telling me how to help her.

I learned that Heather's after-school melt-down pattern was a typical charactersitic of Asperger's. She knew that she needed to act a certain way out in public and would fight to maintain that control but once she was home, she imploded into a shut-down sleep state. She didn't even get up to eat. If I tried to wake her, she couldn't talk in sequential order. It was unbelievable. I went back to Pediatrician "B" and begged for help. I was watching my daughter deteriorate before my eyes. She'd dropped weight; her skin looked pasty-white, as if almost transparent, and had dark circles under her eyes.This was not right!

I explained to Pediatrician "B" that we couldn't go to the social worker//therapist whom he recommended because of our insurance. We found a social worker in Whitewater who was covered by our insurance. This person referred us to Dr. Child Psychologist in Burlington. After working with him for a time, he diagnosed Asperger's Syndrome (AS) and recommended more medication. From a parent's point of view, you don't want to medicate but clearly this child was terribly depressed. Heather and I were fighting so much of the time because of her defiance.

With this child psychologist and family counseling, I learned that I was a safe-zone offering unconditional love for Heather. She held herself together until she got to her safe-zone. It was strenous living day to day as I watched and loved this beautiful little girl who, clearly, had no control over her behaviors. During the "lost years", I was a phone call away and would drop everything to get to her before she shut down completely. She was smart enough to know how to act in public. It may have looked to others like she had control but she didn't. Some friends who were closely involved with this situation thought that it was bad parenting and not Autism. It was never my first choice to put my child on pharmaceuticals but what other choice was there when your child is not functioning? During this time, I noticed that two or three days per month the foggy clouds lifted. She functioned better and was more connected until that fog rolled in again.

Dr. Child Psychologist from Burlington had been trying to contact Pediatrician "B" to no avail. Pediatrician "B" refused to speak to Heather's doctor in Burlington. He wouldn't return any phone call, answer any letters, or respond to him in any way. When I questioned the Pediatrician about this, he explained to me that there was nothing wrong with Heather; she did not have Asperger's. He said that kids with this condition don't make eye contact but Heather could. He should have asked if she **always** made eye contact because with some of the odd little behaviors that Heather had when she was younger, she made no eye contact. My good friends, Betsy and Honey in New Jersey (mothers, educators, and very knowledgeable), told me that if you touch a child under the chin, you can teach them to make eye contact. And when you address them, make sure they're looking at you in the eyes. I made everybody do this; my father, my mother, my husband, and myself. I even asked her Pre-School teachers and Day Care Providers to do this. I'd stop people and tell them that they couldn't talk to her unless they made eye contact. I got down to her level, touched her under her chin, and lifted her face gently. There were times when I laid on the ground and looked up at Heather to make eye contact when we played.

At a young age, I had the experience of observing peoples' body language in a big city near my home in New Jersey. We learned to be tough, walk strong, and make good eye contact because if you didn't, you could get bullied. Plus, it was good manners to look at someone while they were talking. We painstakingly taught Heather to do that. We worked diligently with her for a couple of years and she **did** learn to make eye contact. Pediatrician "B" wasn't listening and still refused to talk to Dr. Child Psychologist. My child was still having melt-downs. She clearly needed help. Why wouldn't this Pediatrician speak to the Child Psychologist? He told me it was because I was a bad mother. Heather wasn't functioning and she was in the closet because I was a bad mother. I was hysterical. I took Heather and left. I was furious! I went to the hospital patient liaison and told her I was appalled at those remarks. Pediatrician "B" wouldn't even speak to the Child Psychologist. How was he looking out for Heather's best interest? I explained that Pediatrician "B" recommended in writing that we go to a mental health therapist/social worker. We did. He recommended medication changes but refused to prescribe anything. We were assigned another pediatrician by the hospital patient liaison. The next day, I went to see Pediatrician "C" from Medical Facility "B". Upon walking in the door, he told me that I was a bad parent and that there was nothing wrong with Heather. He didn't look at me; he didn't look at Heather. I was angry and upset! He was obviously defending his colleague.

I didn't know what to do so I went to my Family Practitioner and explained the whole situation to her. She told me that she didn't know a lot about Asperger's and wanted the weekend to read through some information on it. On Monday, she called and told me that she would prescribe a low dosage of an anti-depressant and suggested that I find an appropriate doctor as soon as I could.

Running parallel with this story was the escalation of Heather's tic. If we touched her, she wouldn't react or respond. Though it didn't last real long, it lasted long enough that there were many pregnant pauses when you were with Heather. We learned from Dr. Child Psychologist in Burlington that during these tics, she was tracing numbers or letters in her head and couldn't move on until she had done it perfectly. We noticed that anxiety made it worse. When she was excited about something, it was worse; scared about something, it was worse; fatigued, it was worse.

I have a family friend, Dr. Laird, who is in medical research. He has a very well-known reputation and has written many books and papers. I happened to be visiting him in Chicago with Heather and my husband, Stan. While out to dinner, Dr. Laird had time to observe Heather. I'd talked to him previously about the testing that had been done so I brought along a copy of the blood work and x-rays that were done by the Pediatrician. Dr. Laird explained to us that the blood work was done at too superficial of a level and what he was observing as a tic, was instead, seizure behavior. He thought I should have additional testing done to evaluate what was really going on with the blood work. The results, though convoluted, had to do with the Pituitary Gland. This gland is the mother-board for five chemicals or hormones produced in the body. Heather's tests showed elevated levels of these hormones which was an indication that there was an imbalance. Further testing was required. So I went to see an endocrinologist at Medical Facility "B" and explained that I was really there for my daughter. I described the situation and brought Dr. Laird's credentials along with his suggestions for different testing. Dr. Endocrinologist said it made perfect sense. These two professionals spoke the same language so the testing was done. They found that Heather produced life-threatening levels of ACTH adrenal stress hormone. There was no endocrine protocol to correct it. There was no medicine of which they knew to remedy this problem. It was sort of an anomaly but it was "life-threatening levels". I have a medical report from Dr. Laird dated October 17, 2001 outlining this information and he recommends, "Any and all efforts should be made to reduce Heather's stress levels".

We were still dealing with Heather's deterioration as we still didn't know how to help her. I needed medical answers, now! I wasn't sure of what to do or where to go. I started networking. I called everywhere: The Madison Autism Chapter, the Milwaukee Autism

Chapter, the main office in Maryland for the Autism Society of America, different school districts to ask for suggestions, and Betsy and Honey, my godparent educators in New Jersey. I sought to get answers and make some intellectual decisions that would be appropriate for my daughter based on information that I was clearly not qualified or trained to understand. I needed to move forward.

In the meantime, Dr. Laird had made a phone call to an old medical school buddy who was married to a doctor at the UW Waisman Center (Developmental Research Center) and she specialized in diagnosing Autistic Spectrum Disorders. He suggested we try there.

I went back to Pediatrician "B" and asked if he had evaluated for anything other than ADD? I also asked to see Heather's health record. I had learned that Asperger's is a developmental disorder so I wanted to know if he had even looked at that possibility. Why wouldn't he look at that? His response was to dismiss us as patients and tell us to seek help elsewhere. I left my insurance plan and returned to my original Pediatrician "A" who gave me the original diagnosis of ADD. At this point, we had three diagnoses of ADD/ADHD and none of the prescribed medications were working. I don't want to speak for this doctor but I think he was surprised when he saw Heather's decline. I brought him up to date and explained that I needed a pediatric referral to the UW Waisman Center for a second opinion. He agreed and made the referral. We booked an appointment and waited for months.

The doctor at the UW Waisman Center did Heather's evaluations. The result was a second diagnosis of Mild-High-Functioning Autism, Asperger's Syndrome. She then referred me to a neuro-psychologist in the UW system that provided a list of recommendations for school and suggestions for some medical supports. The neuro-psychologist explained that Heather's inattentiveness was her Autism and referred us to a therapist/social worker and a psychiatrist with medication suggestions. Based on those suggestions, we sought to find people that could help us.

> *If you start using medication in a person with Autism, you should see obvious improvement in behavior in a short period of time. If you do not see obvious improvement, they probably should not be taking the stuff. It's that simple.*
>
> – *Temple Grandin*

I also tried to get organized. **Here is Tip #2: Get two folders each with separate pockets. Mark one for Education and the other for Medical.** The tip I'm giving you is to get two folders each with separate pockets. You will want to separate those pockets based on the different aspects of the characteristics. I want to give this tip to you now because the sooner you get organized; the better it will be as you riffle through all the paper work. You'll be inundated so organization is really the key.

For continuity, I will outline the mental health role through Heather's High School years. Armed with the information I had and because Heather, due to an insurance change, was missing so much school, I found the names of a local therapist/social worker and a psychiatrist that claimed to have experience with Autism. They were part of the same Medical Facility as Pediatrician "A" so I felt better. The therapist/ social worker saw Heather a number of times and then called us in for a family session. She informed us that she "didn't see Asperger's". I learned later that kids with Asperger's do well one-on-one with adults; they have issues with peers. At that time and because Heather liked this therapist, I sent a letter to her stating that we had brought two diagnoses of AS; one of which, from the much respected Waisman Center. I asked her to not question the diagnosis but to work on the self-esteem and socialization issues.

A month later, we saw the psychiatrist. Two months prior, when I made the appointment, I delivered all of the medical records from the Waisman Center, including the neuro-psychologist's recommendations for medication. Heather sat on the floor looking at books while I talked to the psychiatrist. She asked why I had made the appointment. I explained that it was based on the recommendations from the Waisman Center for medication for AS. During these ten minutes, she didn't ask me a single question. She didn't look at or ask Heather a single question. This woman told me that I was a bad mother who was using Heather like a specimen and that she didn't have AS. I told her that she didn't have to believe me. I asked her if she had read the medical records which I had delivered from the Waisman Center. She informed me that she didn't have to read them if I was bringing Heather in for medication; she had to do her own evaluation. I asked her why she didn't speak to Heather's Pediatrician "A" who had all of her up-dated medical information and was in the same Medical Facility. I was handed evaluation forms which needed to be completed if I wanted any prescriptions. These forms were the same forms I completed six years prior with Pediatrician "A". The billing office submitted insurance for ADD because the psychiatrist based her diagnosis "on the information she was provided during the appointment". Needless to say, this was a step backwards. I started looking for another psychiatrist. I wasn't really surprised when I received a letter from the Therapist/Social Worker terminating therapy "due to the medical complexity of the case".

I found a very qualified professional in Elkhorn (a forty-five minute drive away) who never questioned the diagnosis. She effectively worked with Heather through High School on self-esteem and socialization issues. Heather's raging behaviors toward me gradually subsided and communication improved between us especially during emotional situations. We worked on body language and tone of voice versus the words used. Heather's new psychiatrist worked in this facility one day per month. She was from Milwaukee and specialized in girls on the Autism Spectrum. This was the beginning of our roller coaster ride of different anti-depressants and anxiety medications. Nothing worked and some made it much worse. We eventually found a more effective solution than medication!

Here's Tip #3: When securing medical coverage for your child with Autism, the diagnosis should come from a medical doctor, MD. If the diagnosis is made by a Mental Health Provider, PhD, your insurance will only cover mental health supports. With the MD diagnosis, it opens the door for coverage in OT, PT, and SLP.

> *The difference between high-functioning autism and low-functioning autism is that high-functioning means your deficits are ignored and low-functioning autism means your assets are ignored.*
>
> *– Laura Tisoncik*
> *Circle of Moms Blog*

CHAPTER 3

SPD [Sensory Processing Disorder]
Does Anyone Speak My Daughter's Language?

> *Sensory Processing Disorder is the inability to use information received through the senses in order to function smoothly in daily life.*
>
> <u>The Out of Sync Child</u>
> – Carol Stock Kranowitz

Does This Explain Heather?

THROUGH NETWORKING, I read about Sensory Integration as it was termed in the 1990's. Now referred to as Sensory Processing Disorder (SPD), I will use this terminology throughout the remainder of this book.

I had never heard of SPD but through my networking, searching for supports for Autism, how to evaluate a child, and reading anything I could find, Sensory Processing Disorder continued to surface.

As I mentioned in Chapter One, we lived in many states due to my husband's career. I have friends and family in New Jersey, Texas, Florida, and California. I called everyone. I spoke to anyone who would listen: Have you ever heard of this? What are they doing? How do you help your child? I would take note when a parent talked about an aspect of their child that was similar to Heather; I wanted to learn more about it. What are they doing? Do you have Functioning Recovery? What is that? How does that happen? I continued to look for answers.

I sought answers from every parent who had a child with Functioning Recovery. I kept hearing about supports: Sensory Processing and one called Neuro-Biological Supports now called Bio-Medical Therapies. (I'll discuss these further in this chapter.) I was inundated with different therapies used for different kids. Some of these I would read and say, "Gee, that's not really Heather" and others I would say, "Oh, now **that's** more like Heather". I had to accept that this was her diagnosis. It didn't really matter what we called it, what mattered more was what we could do to help her. Everyone deals with something. We had to accept the situation and move forward. So this is "growing up Heather"? At this point, all added up, Heather had a whole umbrella of disabilities: Asperger's Syndrome (AS) [a syndrome meaning a set of symptoms characterizing a disease] and an Autistic Spectrum Disorder (ASD) [her symptoms included ADD, ADHD, OCD, and ODD]. She also had phantom rashes, severe allergies, the seizure/tics, and issues with socialization. I organized structured play-dates for Heather like a horseback riding trip or a trip to the theater but there was no free play. She could not and did not want that. The older she got the more isolated she was from her peers. There were no teenage friends who called to go to the movies or to shop. The mall was not an environment she enjoyed. Heather was High-Functioning so as I talk about her, it almost appears or sounds like this could be any other neuro-typical teenager but I couldn't deny that something wasn't right. Even her allergies were extreme and debilitating. Her eyes swelled shut preventing her from leaving the house.

The Asperger's diagnosis fit and was greatly affecting her ability to function at school. How do I fix that? How do I help her medically?

I quit my full time job when Heather was in Eighth Grade. I had a simple set of rules: I worked, so she was with her older brother for a couple of hours until I got home; unless there was bleeding, throwing up, running a high fever, or the house was on fire, she wasn't allowed to call me. Yet, Heather would incessantly call me at work; over and over and over. I remember being in my office holding the phone with my boss sitting next to me who rolled his eyes. I would ask, "Are you bleeding? Is someone breaking in the house? You cannot call me at work". She would call me about non-important issues over and over again. I told her to get a snack, get ready for dance class, and I would pick her up at 4:15 pm and yet when I got there she was not nearly ready and she was zoned out. Heather was not making it. I was overwhelmed with trying to find help and keeping her functioning. It's a kid's job to go to school: get up in the morning, get dressed, brush their teeth, eat, and go to school. Then they should come home, do their homework, play with friends, etc. Not in Heather's world. I quit my job to focus on Heather and I read, researched, and attended seminars. I started to read books on Asperger's and interventions for Asperger's and Autism. I happened to be on a business trip with my husband; there was a conference in North Carolina on Autism. I crashed it. I gathered every piece of information that I could about what was going on. That facility had a lot of information from the Yale Child Study Group and the New England Children's Institute. I read, got online, and contacted them for more information.

While in New Jersey visiting my family, I visited The Autism Research Institute in Princeton to gather more information. I went to different support groups in different states and spoke to different parents as were my friends, the educators. SPD information kept speaking to me as I gathered more information. I read a book called <u>The Out of Sync Child </u>by Carol Stock-Kranowitz and I said," This is Heather! This is what's going on with Heather!" *(Refer to Appendix D for Books)*

It talked about the odd behaviors, not wanting to be touched, auditory processing issues, the food issues, and the smell issues. I learned about touch differences. For example: Heather didn't like to be touched but she could touch others. She would come up behind me and she'd squeeze me like I was a teddy bear. She used deep, hard pressure as if trying to squeeze out the stuffing. We learned that these behaviors are typical for someone with SPD.

I knew the school had an Occupational Therapist (OT) so I referred Heather for an evaluation. The school OT administered the Dunn Sensory Profile; I, of course, sat in on the evaluation. The OT pointed out differences to me. What she saw made a lot of sense to me regarding Heather. She casually commented that I should get another opinion. This OT appeared to understand certain things about Heather; I was hopeful that she would provide suggestions to help. At the school's Individual Education Plan (IEP) referral meeting for Special Education she commented, "Whatever Mom was doing was working and no support was needed." At the end of the meeting, I asked the OT about the information she mentioned at the evaluation. Again, she suggested I get another opinion.

Let me tell you how hard it was to find someone to evaluate my child for SPD. I was turned down by every OT in the county where I live in. I couldn't get anyone to do an evaluation. I was willing to pay cash. "Please evaluate her. I think this is important." One local facility told me I had to resolve the issue with the School District before they would evaluate Heather. How did they know I was having an issue with the School District? I was turned away from Madison trying to get an evaluation. I booked an appointment with an OT in Milwaukee's Children's Hospital for an evaluation. When we got there and they saw how old Heather was, they turned us away. No one was willing to evaluate a child almost thirteen years old with a new diagnosis of Asperger's. Milwaukee gave me the name, Sue Kratz. They said that she was very knowledgeable and had even trained occupational therapists in some school districts. We made an appointment with Sue Kratz, OTR, BCP, Developmental Therapies, Inc. and now Special Therapies, Inc. in Waukesha.

> *I cannot emphasize enough the importance of a good teacher.*
>
> *– Temple Grandin*

We started with Ms. Kratz on September 26, 2001. I explained that an evaluation had been done at the school and they noted, "She may have some sensory differences" but according to the school, these were not affecting her educational performance so no supports were needed. Ms. Kratz wanted to see the evaluation from the school. After ample letter writing, they finally agreed to release it.

Ms. Kratz explained how the Dunn Sensory Profile evaluates the child. A portion of the test is subjective which then leads the therapist to do observational work in order to draw conclusions. Ms. Kratz used the school's subjective portion of the evaluation then did her own observational work to draw her own conclusions. She completed her evaluation and wrote her conclusions and recommendations for the school (January 15, 2001). Ms. Kratz found that Heather indeed had Sensory Processing Dysfunction which had been unaddressed for many years. Heather was broken down and was exhibiting sensory issues like that of a three year old toddler. I was floored. Was this why she wasn't functioning at school? This was a serious issue. Ms. Kratz spoke Heather's language and she became my interpreter. If she referenced a book, I bought it. If she mentioned a seminar, I attended it.

I learned that there are actually seven sensory systems in the body. Most of us know the five senses that we learned in Kindergarten: see (visual), smell (olfactory), taste (Gustatory), hear (auditory), and touch (tactile) but there are two hidden systems; vestibular (sense of balance) and proprioception (where you are positioned in space). To clarify, your visual system is responsible for visual stimulation; the malfunction could show hyper-focus on objects. They crave more visual stimulation and can stare for hours. Olfactory system interprets the environment by smell. The malfunction makes eating certain foods intolerable. The Gustatory system function interprets food by taste and the malfunction creates eating difficulties. The auditory system interprets speech and sounds in the environment. The malfunction can be super-hearing. They can't filter sounds to focus on the teacher or what's important. The tactile system is responsible for exploration and defense from harm. Malfunction can be over registration and can resemble fight-or-flight because the body becomes defensive when it perceives a non-threatening touch as threatening. The child may not be aware they were touched so they have a high tolerance for pain. Think of a child who couldn't feel the touch of a hot pan. A child could be a sensory-seeker pursuing or craving deeper pressure to their body. These children can be thrill seekers; their need for it clouds their judgment regarding safety issues. The vestibular system function is input from body movement and movement in the environment. It provides unconscious information about the body's state of balance. It is usually developed by two months old and is the driving force between all the other senses. Malfunction occurs when the body over registers, under registers, or a combination of both regarding the information about the environment in which they live. Maladaptive behaviors can occur in an effort to compensate for the excess or lack of vestibular stimulation. Lack, a child may run, rock or pace, a child with excess may lean, slump or shuffle, attempting to avoid contact with others. The Proprioceptive System function allows for accurate motor planning and provides body awareness. Good function allows for smooth movements by providing information about where the body begins or ends; its location in space. Malfunction results when the body is unable to conceptualize, plan, or execute a motor plan activity. This can hinder interactions with others.

Heather was broken down to the vestibular level and one system effects how the other systems work. I remember when Heather was a child of six or seven years old, we'd go out into the snow. I'd put on her snow pants, snow boots, snow coat, hat, and mittens and she'd fall over. We couldn't hold her up. We use to laugh about it back then. This was Heather's world. I would try to hold her up by her collar but she couldn't stay standing. If we got her outside, we would get her to walk a little bit but a few minutes later we would just see her lying flat on her back in the snow. She couldn't walk while wearing all those clothes.

Things started to make sense. I enrolled Heather in ballet because she was clumsy, she didn't have good control over her movements, and dancing with the music helped. She stumbled a lot. Toddlers stumble when they learn to walk but Heather still looked like that when she was four and five years old.

I think of all the times that I disciplined Heather. I bring this up because it's normal to ask your child to clean her room and when they don't do it, they get a time-out, go without dessert, or miss their favorite TV show. Heather had some of those consequences. Ms. Kratz explained to me how the vestibular system affects Heather. Every movement Heather made took motor planning. It was amazing what her brain had to go through to reach out to get something. The motor planning that was involved to pick up an object, move it into the toy chest, and then move onto the next object was very taxing on her system. I would put Heather in her room and tell her to come out when it was clean. Every time I checked on her progress, she was passed out, in a shut-down state, in the middle of that un-cleaned room. Now, I understood. I couldn't continue to discipline her for something she wasn't able to do. I learned to pick my battles. I bought a shovel for indoors. I shoveled a clear path so if Heather got up in the middle of the night she wouldn't hurt herself. Cleaning her room caused Heather to rage at me even more and I still couldn't get her to clean her own room. I was exasperated much of the time.

Ms. Kratz talked about how these kids can't adapt to situations. Their systems didn't have the right coping strategies and that some kids actually had seizures. Our job as parents, she advised, was to try to seek out how our child functions. We needed to be detectives so we could understand why and from where those behaviors were originating. She talked about how the sensory piece affected the brain; inflammations, toxins, metabolic disturbances. She talked about how it affected the nervous system and that for some kids who have a short fuse, they're fine one minute and then they're in a rage or a melt-down the next. They can't modulate their systems. Their system is wired to overreact to basic sensory events. She talked about kids having problems moving or planning to move. They watched other kids on the monkey bars but they might not want to be on that equipment because they couldn't figure out how their bodies were supposed to function. She talked about a condition called Dyspraxia and why a child can exhibit a skill or some educational knowledge one day or time of the day, but not another, based on their sensory state.

For some children, there is no filter to modulate what they're thinking and feeling; no self-regulation. There were social-emotional ramifications. It could affect the child's ability to clothe themselves. For the same reason, you could line up ten children with the same diagnosis of Autism; mild Asperger's for instance, and see ten different presentations. You could line up ten children with SPD and see ten different presentations. Like Autism, SPD was on a continuum. There are milder or more severe forms. I believe Ms. Kratz referred to it as Behavioral Neurology. Children behave a particular way because of their neurological system and how they're wired. Sensory processing is the taking-in of stimulation, the body's ability to process that stimulation, and then your body's ability to effectively respond.

Therapy with Ms. Kratz was consistent and ongoing. We tried to go every two weeks and maintained that schedule for approximately four years. We learned that Heather's food issues were part of it and she probably ate the same foods because of how they felt going down her throat. During the "lost years", rigidity at its worst, she ate Hot and Sour Soup four to five days a week at a cost of $3.15 per quart. We recognized the need to set parameters but to not impede on some sensory demands unless it endangered her or others. She had tried to hurt herself and that was simply not an option or ever going to be tolerated so we continued to address that issue with her Social Worker/Therapist as well as with the sensory supports. We would have done anything to stop that behavior. There were no excuses for self-abuse. We learned to set perimeters. As long as it was healthy and all natural, she could eat as much as she wanted. The more Ms. Kratz learned about Heather, the more **we** learned about Heather. For instance, in Middle School, Heather insisted on wearing dance clothing to school; Bali Togs and Danskin (Lycra included). We learned that the spandex gives deep pressure to the body so Heather gravitated to that attire.

Ms. Kratz was teaching us how to be "detectives" in how our child functions. What preceded the behaviors? What were the triggers? We became good detectives. First we discovered the signs Heather had when she was escalating. It was hard to figure out at first but over time we began to notice things; her shoulders elevated, her skin color paled or turned ashen, and dark circles appeared around her eyes. Her ability to be around people lessened and the tic escalated. When her system was off, we noticed that she became clumsier or had less ability to regulate herself. Her speech and tone sounded urgent and she couldn't control it. When she got up in the morning it could take two to three hours for her to feel like she could walk erect or converse when asked a question. We also learned that to have SPD was like having the body stuck in a fight-or-flight mode. There are two aspects of the Central Nervous System: the sympathetic nervous system and the parasympathetic nervous system. This sympathetic nervous system sends signals to the body to flee. It is in a heightened state of alertness. The parasympathetic nervous system sends signals to the body to rest, relax, and digest. Heather was stuck in that fight-or-flight mode. In this mode, all the nutrients and signals to the body are used to prepare the body to defend itself. None of these nutrients are used to sustain the body's health. This is extremely taxing on the human body which explains Heather's drastic weight loss.

Upon recommendation, we administered an auditory desensitization program to improve auditory processing. It was an eight-week program with a CD for each week. Heather listened to a CD for a week for fifteen minutes, two times a day with special headphones that went over the ears and blocked out all other noise. We saw changes in her behaviors, sometimes more rage, sometimes more melt-downs but sometimes a level of balance. Heather also started verbalizing that she was feeling parts of her head or brain for the first time. Here's that heightened sensitivity again. Heather had previously told me that she could feel the food digest in her stomach or when aspirin hit her blood stream. Heather revisited this listening program many times over the years and music is still an integral part of her driving skills. Heather now knows if her system is at a certain point, she can't drive. Those times are few and far between but thank goodness she recognizes it.

Upon recommendation, we administered a brushing program which was developed by Patricia Wilbarger, MeD, OTR, and FAOTA. This program was designed to decrease sensory or tactile defensiveness. Brushing the skin balanced the sense of touch. We used a surgical brush to brush the skin. We were supposed to brush the entire body but Heather only tolerated this treatment for short amounts of time. I was too rough; she was so sensitive I couldn't seem to lighten up enough to help Heather so she did as much as she could tolerate. Children with tactile defensiveness had difficulty transitioning between activities or were lethargic. Ms. Kratz documented Heather as Sedentary. Currently she can tolerate touch much better and even enjoys and derives benefit from a massage. Before this, she wouldn't have been able to tolerate this type of touch.

By Ninth Grade, Heather had given up Dance Class. She would go to school or to Dance Class but she wasn't physically up to do both. The natural progression for ballet is dancing on point shoes. With Heather's vestibular system being off, point dancing was exceedingly difficult for her and she couldn't progress like the other students. The socialization aspect of dance became an issue as well. She just couldn't keep up with her peers nor understood social cues. She was always upset about someone. She could socialize but socialization caused greater self-isolation.

During this Eighth and Ninth Grade phase, Heather was broken down and in the cubby-hole in her closet for hours each day. I noticed a few things. One: I could go into the closet with her but if I sat too far away she would never acknowledge my presence. If I sat too close, I could escalate the situation. Sometimes I could get close enough to somehow join her space but not invade it. I could engage her with simple yes-no questions. Are you in pain? At that time she didn't have a lot of body awareness. She couldn't tell me if anything hurt. Do you think you'll need to be in here a long time? Should I stay with you? Is there something you need? If there was something she needed, it was usually the blanket she received the day she was born on March 7th, 1987 and still has today. In Middle School, she was asked about her most prized possession; it was that blanket. If it calmed her down, I was good with it. I wanted her out of that cubby-hole closet. At this point, if I dragged her out, she would lay on the floor crying for hours.

The next recommendation was for CranioSacral Therapy (CST). What did she just say? Cranio what? Sacral who? Ms. Kratz explained that this therapy had been emerging over the past thirty years to improve overall function of the central nervous system. There were parallels to sensory integration, the function of the cranial system, and how these impairments appeared in what sensory differences that children presented. My homework was the CranioSacral System and brain functioning. How do you say sphenoid? I learned that Dr. John Upledger was considered the Father of CranioSacral Therapy. He founded the Upledger Institute in 1985 and shortly thereafter developed a one-week intensive treatment program for children with Autism. It is still open today. I learned that it improved sensory, motor, and mental dysfunction. I read Dr. Upledger's published paper. On April 6, 2000, he appeared before the government Reform Committee of the U.S. House Of Representatives, 106th Congress (1999-2000). It featured testimonies from leaders in the field of research and treatment for Autism and included parents of children with Autism. Dr. Upledger believed some of the behaviors he observed in Autistic children were attempts to change or correct physiological and/or anatomical dysfunction that might be causing pain or discomfort. "Many children bang their head, chew on their wrists and /or the bases of their thumbs until deep tissue (tendon sheath) is visible, and/ or they may suck on their thumbs so vigorously that the upper teeth begin to displace forward".

Hmmmmm! Heather had some physiological anomalies and she liked to push up on the roof of her mouth. We asked Ms. Kratz to facilitate CranioSacral Therapy. By this time, we hadn't been able to touch Heather in close to four years. She was so sensitive, we could not kiss her on the cheek; she backed away. I kissed her hairline because she could tolerate it there. I learned to appreciate the scent of her hair rather than the feel of her cheek. Her skin did not respond normally to things. If it was hot outside and Heather was in the sun, where most people would turn red and sunburn, Heather would get swollen eyes and get puffy. She couldn't go outside in really cold weather. Her cheeks would actually get chapped. Most people have chapped lips but these would be her cheeks and they would split. It was very uncomfortable for her.

Let me tell you what it looked like to watch the facilitation of CST. Heather lay face-up on the table and Ms. Kratz put her hands and/or her fingers on various parts of her head, neck, shoulders, back, legs, and inside her mouth. During some sessions, she kept her hands in one place for an extended period of time. That's it. Heather felt "nothing". At the conclusion of the session, Heather would be exceedingly tired and slept for eight to twelve hours. The child who woke up was different. There was clarity for Heather; some of the fog had cleared. It was like a break in the storm. It lasted for a few days then some of the symptoms returned. After some time, Heather asked for CST. She began to tell Ms. Kratz which bones needed work. We noticed a change in the symmetry of Heather's forehead. If it looked a certain way, we recognized her need for therapy. The first time Heather had mouth work, she responded that her tongue "fit in her mouth for the first time". She was calmer and the seizure/tic subsided. When Heather had work done in her mouth, the technique to relieve restrictions in her cranial base was the same movement she was doing when she was pushing her fingers on the roof of her mouth. Interesting! It was in the area of her head where the poorly-working pituitary gland was; the gland responsible for her stress producing hormone levels.

This therapy plays such a role for Heather. She continues to receive it and will for the rest of her life. Heather has also learned a CST technique called "still-point" so she can self-access when she needs it. It helps to calm her and reorganizes her central nervous system.

I remember being surprised when Heather got off the table after her third and fourth CST session and spontaneously hugged me. Two arms wrapped around my shoulders while she was facing me. I could feel her heart rate through my chest and her cheek on my cheek. She said, "Thank you!" I hadn't had a hug like that in ages. Heather continues to derive benefits from CST and I have seen some amazing results with children including non-verbal children beginning to speak during a session.

Another effective recommendation from Ms. Kratz was Bio-Medical Therapies.

I first attended a seminar by Dr. Jeffrey Bradstreet, Director ICDRC, and International Child Development Research Center. He talked about the work of Dr. Bernard Rimland, The Autism Research Institution. This is my interpretation of what I learned: Every person has a base-line chemical foundation in their body. Children with Autism are missing that base-line chemical foundation like that of their neuro-typical normal peers and a common pattern of imbalance is being seen amongst children on the Autism Spectrum. For instance, most lack serotonin, a brain neuro-transmitter. This chemical helps maintain the connections in the brain. Other common deficit chemicals in children with Autistic Spectrum Disorders include folic acid, magnesium, B vitamin, and B complex vitamin to name few.

Dr. Bradstreet's suggestions were to test hair, blood, saliva, urine and stool to evaluate what chemicals were missing, chelate (remove) mercury from vaccinations, and replace what was missing. He was located in Florida; we needed someone closer.

Dr. Bradstreet also talked about the role of vaccines and Autism. The build-up of mercury was poisonous to a child. I started thinking about the vaccine picture. I saw a decline in Heather after her two-year-old shots and again in Fifth Grade after a Hepatitis B vaccine. My gut told me this information was relevant. We already knew Heather had an issue with her hormone levels.

I started to look at what was happening with Autism. When I first heard Heather's diagnosis in 2000, prevalence was 1 in 450 children were suspected to fall on the Autistic Spectrum. Then the Center for Disease Control (CDC) announced 1 in 235, then 1 in 150 and now, 1 in 88. Heather's diagnosis was twelve years ago. I'm not anti-vaccine but I have questions. In 1987, twelve vaccines were recommended by the American

Medical Association (AMA). That number has more than tripled; add yearly flu shots and the new vaccines that are frequently recommended. Has anyone looked at what the increase, with the number of vaccines administered, is doing to our children? Is there a correlation between the increases in prevalence of Autism with the increase of recommended vaccinations? **Based on the CDC's recommended vaccine schedule for 2012, your child may receive up to 81 vaccinations by the age of six. These numbers do not reflect the recommendations for certain populations and there are currently over two hundred additional vaccines in development.** Children may not need to be vaccinated at all. There is a test called the Titers Test. It measures the amount and presence of antibodies in the blood. Based on the results of a Titers Test, you would vaccinate **only** for what antibodies are missing. If the child already has immunity to a disease then why vaccinate for it? I know families who have had the Titers Test administered and they only needed to vaccinate their child for one disease. Again, why administer a vaccine if the child already has the immunity?

The vaccine-Autism link is highly controversial. It is best to do your own research. My research helped me draw my conclusions. One article really struck me. I read <u>Deadly Immunity</u> written by Robert F. Kennedy. Jr. dated June 16, 2005. He is an advocate who set out to set the record straight regarding the implication that vaccines cause Autism. It is an eleven page article that discusses the government's role in testing. Robert F. Kennedy Jr. writes, "When a study revealed that mercury in childhood vaccines may have caused Autism in thousands of kids, the government rushed to conceal the data and prevent parents from suing drug companies for their role in the epidemic". I read additional articles and case studies but it's a personal choice. I also know I vaccinated my child and something happened; she was not the same. My personal choice was to no longer allow the vaccines to be administered to my children. <u>Www.GenerationRescue.com</u> is a good website providing case studies of children; those vaccinated versus those not vaccinated.

About ten months later, Ms. Kratz found and referred Heather to a Pediatrician who did Bio-Medical Therapies, Dr. John Hicks, Pathways Medical Advocates in Greys Lake, Illinois. Greys Lake was a two and a half hour drive each way from our home which we could certainly do. We made an appointment. I forwarded Heather's medical records so he had a thorough medical history. He had hair, blood, saliva, urine, and stool-testing done. I won't be able to accurately detail the results, due to its complexity and scientific terms, but I will try to explain as simply as possible. Dr. Hicks gave me a one-inch-thick notebook with explanations of why and what he was testing. They were evaluating Heather's chemical foundation in her body. There were forty-one different amino acids alone and we have twenty-plus pages of different chemical results. Dr. Hicks figured out which chemicals Heather was missing and what was causing her allergies. Then, they systematically replaced what was missing, changed the diet so the child is no longer consuming certain foods, and removed (chelated) the mercury.

I explained to Dr. Hicks that I tried to put Heather on a casein and gluten free diet but she got worse.[Casein is a protein found in cow's milk which is difficult to digest and believed to cause behavior problems in children with Autism.] A casein gluten-free diet kept coming up as a support for children with Autism. He explained that it was like putting the cart ahead of the horse. When omitting gluten from a child's diet, it is usually replaced with rice. Heather was allergic to rice. I did not have her on the appropriate elimination diet. He also explained that a child could be externally allergic and internally allergic to things. Heather had traditional allergy testing which showed her allergies to grass, flowers, plants, trees, bushes, shrubs, and all tree bearing fruit. Now that we knew that she was allergic to rice, seafood, milk, etc. these were eliminated from her diet. We also learned that Heather had no serotonin in her body. Apparently without serotonin, Zoloft and most of the anti-depressants would never help. These drugs, known as "re-up take inhibitors", are designed to take your body's production of serotonin from the adrenals and bring it up to the brain. Prior to this,

Heather had never been checked to see if she produced serotonin. Dr. Hicks explained that Heather could clinically overdose on Zoloft and it would never help her because she produced no serotonin. He weaned her off the medication.

Also important, he explained the brain's ability to correct itself. If the chemical imbalances were corrected before the child turned eighteen years old or stopped growing, the brain could jump-start and begin to produce the chemicals it needed. He told us that Heather had Serotonin Disorder, Neuro-transmitter Disorder, and an Immune Disorder. He prescribed an appropriate elimination diet, recommended seventeen different daily vitamins and minerals, and an IV injection once per month.

He was right! A year later, we had a very different child. She improved physiologically. She no longer looked ashen or pale, she looked stronger and healthier. The depression symptoms improved. The nervousness and anxiety subsided. Environments which Heather couldn't handle still left her in a melt-down state but not for the usual five days nor to that intensity. With this improvement, Heather began to eat some of the foods which previously caused an allergic reaction. I remember celebrating that she could eat part of an orange with no reaction; she was sixteen years old.

We continued working with Ms. Kratz while doing all of the other therapies. As long as we were moving forward, getting answers, and learning ways to help Heather, we continued. These "out of the box", non-traditional therapies were proving to be most helpful. We learned information that reflected Heather; things which told us what great things she had to offer, how to work with her, and what areas needed help. I was on-board whether insurance covered it or not. I fought with the insurance company for two years to get insurance coverage for OT supports.

I want to include some additional information regarding insurance. I gave you a previous tip (Tip #3 in Chapter Two) about getting a diagnosis for Autism and making sure that it came from an MD opposed to a PhD or a Mental Health Provider. I want to give you some more information for the purpose of getting insurance coverage for independent evaluations and Therapies for OT, PT, or SLP because most families have difficulty securing coverage. In the medical domain, they believe that a school-age child doesn't need to have these supports paid for through insurance because those supports are provided by the school. In the educational domain, they have made a decision regarding which aspects of these supports are medical vs. educational. In the Educational Domain the therapist cannot diagnose and draws conclusions based on educational implication only.

Here is how to get around it so that the insurance will provide coverage. Let's use OT as our example.

In writing, request from your school district the medical aspects of the OT supports that are being provided for your child while they're in school. Ask the school to reply to you in writing. Chances are, if they do, they're only going to be able to reply one way. In an educational domain, they do not make medical diagnoses nor do they cover medical aspects of a disability. If you have that piece of paper with you, it's very easy to appeal to your insurance company when your services are denied. You simply write a letter to them and explain that in the educational domain, they do not address the medical aspects of the disability. If you have the letter from the school, it's even better to include that. Do not be afraid to appeal. In our case, Heather was denied as well. At the time, I wasn't aware of the educational-medical domain game that they played. I personally continued to pay for those supports. I went through the appeal process with the insurance company. There are different levels. We were denied in appeals. I appealed again. Notify your insurance company and they will tell you what the procedures are to appeal and what you need to do. With my insurance company, I appealed all the way up to the Doctor's Panel which was just before having to go forward to Mediation. I included a letter and detailed documentation about how the sensory processing piece was helping Heather and ultimately we were able to do away with a lot of expensive medical supports because we were doing this sensory piece. I encourage you to appeal. Find out what that appeals process is and make sure you clearly establish that in the educational domain they do not address any medical aspects of your child's disability. This will open the door for you to get supports for OT, PT, and SLP paid for independently. I strongly recommend that you do this.

I am so grateful! Unlike other therapists, Ms. Kratz was open to having a parent in the room with her. She welcomed the opportunity to help the parents gain tools to use at home. This is a crucial step in understanding how to help your child achieve Functioning Recovery. She wanted the parents to learn.

Here is Tip #4: Any OT, PT, or SLP Professional working with your child, should be willing to have open discussions with you and allow you to observe their work or you should reconsider working with this Professional. You will gain a wealth of information and learn how to work with your child.

I continued to be a 'sensory detective' reporting back to Ms. Kratz. I began to recognize how Heather's sensory needs may be different in different environments. We had a lot of revelations about Heather at that time and we had a lot of revelations as parents. We learned the difference between touching and being touched. Which is why she could come from behind and squeeze us but we couldn't come face to face with her for a hug. We also began to notice signs that Heather was escalating by the tone in her voice and the urgency of her demands. We learned that if she went to a social gathering, she could only tolerate that environment a short amount of time and then she would need to isolate herself afterwards. The melt-down duration and recovery time were different when in an environment like a theater or a musical play vs. socialization or educational.

In 2004, (yes! I'm jumping ahead but I want to be thorough with the sensory information) we were spending a lot of time at Special Therapies, Inc. Ms. Kratz was gathering samples of drawings. She explained that when Science can't do double-blind studies, they gather substantial data over the course of years as one aspect of validation that the therapy in question is helpful. Ms. Kratz explained that they would ask a child to draw a picture of their self. She would then manually apply joint compression for a few minutes. Ms. Kratz would then ask the child to draw a picture of their self again. These before and after pictures were astounding!!!

Before the joint compression

After the joint compression.

Like children on the Autism Spectrum, children with Sensory Processing Disorders could have various degrees and presentations. Heather was like the two drawings above. She could be completely unorganized and not able to display simple skills or she could be very organized and put together. This visual screamed Heather to me. Never was I more convinced that we were on the right path to help Heather achieve Functioning Recovery.

You could see Heather's intellect but she couldn't get it out. Ms. Kratz had a traffic jam game in which cars had to be moved in a certain way to get out of the jam. I couldn't begin to solve the problem but Heather did them at a very high level even though she couldn't explain the steps she took to get to the solution. Even if she did the easy level, she couldn't explain the steps she took. How was she ever going to tell or show how she arrived at mathematical answers if she couldn't get the information out? Ms. Kratz explained that, for every year a child who needs sensory supports and goes without them, it takes twice as long to reeducate them.

Before the joint compression.

Draw A Person

Random

HHt
RS = 5
MA = 4;3

Date: 4/21/11
CA   8;1

"Pretty typical drawing"
per Mom

Goodenough score

After the joint compression.

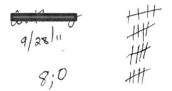

Before

"mad"

After

"passed out but happy"

The greater the fatigue, the greater the Autistic-like characteristics presented. There was a continual, very tenuous balance between education, therapy, and socialization. It got to the point where our world became very small. There were a lot of therapy appointments and a lot of driving. A couple of my favorite resources are 1) www.SIFocus.com. It's a wonderful online magazine which offers suggestions for sensory supports in different environments and the latest in Sensory Diagnosis and supports. I also love 2) www.AboutAutism.com and 3) www.SPDFoundation.org. I was on their website quite often while researching tips and recommendations.

I will discuss the school implication in the next chapter but I want to say that they were not happy. They made innuendos that Heather's education was suffering because she was missing so much school. Attending the therapy sessions during school hours didn't help. Heather couldn't manage 8:00 am to 3:00 pm at school and I was supposed to leave at 3:00 pm to drive one hour and forty minutes to her OT, two and a half hours to the Bio-Medical Supports or forty minutes to her Social Worker. How do you choose between medical therapies and an education? The therapies were crucial for her health and well-being; it was an easy decision.

We were getting answers from these therapies and learning about tools to help Heather. I figured we could always educate Heather after she's healthier. The more we did the sensory supports, the more we saw changes in Heather. First, this phenomenal CranioSacral Therapy not only allowed us to touch her but helped her to control her seizure/tic. Incredible! Heather was involved in a brain imaging study which showed that she does have an imbalance in her cranial bones. I began to look at her forehead as a means for gauging Heather's sensory state. If the bones were protruding I knew this was affecting her focus. If the frontal bones above her eyebrows were protruding, I knew she needed CST.

Ms. Kratz continued to evaluate Heather's functioning ability. We were to look for signs of fatigue even if they were subtle and note if there was a cycle to them. She explored ways to either give Heather energy support when she was beginning to melt down into a shut-down or to help her bring that energy down when she was up too high. It was called a modulation program. Ms. Kratz explained it as a sensory diet. Heather would eventually be able to self-access these supports as she needed them whether we saw signs of the meltdown or not. We began to learn what that was, how to use it, and why it was so important.

We made efforts to provide Heather with a 'safe-haven'; a place she could feel comfortable and get her out of the cubby-hole areas she was seeking. We made attempts to alter our house to allow for sensory things that Heather needed in her home. We made sensory spaces for her. Heather needed bouncing balls, thera-bands for deep pressure, and fiddle toys. Heather was very tactile and needed soft comforters and fabrics and knitted textures. To this day, Heather's favorite item is a receiving blanket that my mother knitted for her. As a newborn, Heather came home from the hospital with this blanket. It still provides great comfort to her even though it is thread-bare and falling apart. Heather needs to touch it, hold it, and have it near her. We redecorated her bedroom into an environment where she felt safe. We painted calm blue walls with puffy white clouds along with flowers and butterflies. We painted the lower half of the room a dark color and also added stars and moons that glowed in the dark. The ceiling was a bright red, yellow, and orange sun. We bought a waterbed so Heather could heat it when she was chilled and couldn't warm her body. She needed five or six blankets on top of her; she had to approve the texture for softness or she wouldn't use it. We gave her a space heater and an extra fan so she could accommodate her temperature needs. We filled her room with sensory supports so she could bounce, rock, fidget, twirl, or jump as she needed. We also purchased a trampoline so she could bounce when desired. There were many times during the "lost years" where Heather couldn't tell us what triggered an episode but we learned to accept that something had happened to her because she sought sensory supports. We learned to give her the time she needed to reorganize her system.

I learned how helpful it was to front-load information so she was prepared to go into certain environments. If we were going somewhere, I learned to have an understanding of what the place would look like. Was it calm or chaotic-looking? How many people would be there? Would it be an organized schedule or open socialization? I had to problem-solve as to how I could make it easier for her to be in that particular environment. Without this preparation, her tic would get out of control, she would disappear, and when I found her she would demand to leave while fighting to keep in-check. Since children with Autism like structure and consistency, we learned to front-load Heather with information regarding changes in her schedule or routines. This helped reduce her anxiety.

I remember learning to accept what I wouldn't have accepted earlier. For instance, my son was a high school wrestler. When we went to his wrestling matches, they were held in gymnasiums that were loud and noisy. If you have never been to a High School Wrestling Match or Meet, they last for hours and parents only get to see their child wrestle for six minutes; maybe longer if attending a Meet. We sat as a group with our wrestling team families. People were everywhere as they yelled and cheered for the wrestlers. This scene mixed with sweaty athletic bodies, food being eaten, and people bumping into each other in tight spaces, was not a good situation. We sat for hours on bleachers watching Justin wrestle but Heather couldn't tolerate that environment. We learned to accept that she was going to be underneath those bleachers. It was quiet under there with no other people around her. She played there with her toys for hours on end. She even ate under there. She could not tolerate it up on top. I really let my child play under dirty bleachers? She showed me how she sat by the wall so the trash and garbage wouldn't drop on her. I had to admit the under-the-bleacher environment made it easier for her.

Ms. Kratz laid out our goals and objectives for Heather's Self-Regulation Program in her evaluation dated January 15th 2002. Heather was 14.10 years of age.

Self-Regulation Program – Goals and Objectives:

Stage One:

1. Recognizing the language and key phases for neurological organization.

2. Adult or therapist labels their current behavior with neurological phases.

3. Client increases awareness of their own neurological states and the difference between: calm/alert/attentive states, increasing stress, reaching overload, modulation vs. un-modulated states.

4. Client identifies and labels states and changing levels of neurological states.

5. Client identifies and labels neurological states outside of therapy environment.

Stage Two:

6. Therapist introduces sensorimotor methods to change/alter neurological states.

7. Therapist identifies sensorimotor preferences and sensory hypersensitivities.

8.   Client begins to experiment with choosing own strategies.

9.   Client chooses strategies independently.

10. Client begins to change neurological states when options are limited (depending on the situation).

11. Client continues to receive support through therapist/family until a satisfactory level of independence and self-regulation is reached.

Ms. Kratz wrote responses observed and parental responses as of January 15, 2002:

1.   Heather has been spontaneously hugging her mother for the first time ever.

2.   Heather is tolerant, seeks and accepts physical closeness now from family members.

3.   Definite positive changes in the amount and duration of "meltdowns" observed at home.

4.   Just beginning The Listening Program.

5.   Has responded to CranioSacral Therapy in the past. Responded quite well to two treatment sessions of this technique provided here. What appeared to be achieved was assisting Heather towards a calm-alert and attentive state and with the emphasis on maintaining that state.

6.   Heather has reached solidly to #4 within Stage One of the Alert Program. She has emerged towards #8 within Stage Two and occasionally some of #9.

We listened to every recommendation Ms. Kratz provided and things started to change. We brushed, we listened to "The Listening Program", used CranioSacral Therapy, and we learned to recognize what was sensory behavior and what was bad behavior. We learned to give Heather consequences for bad behavior at a time when her system **could** handle it. For example, I couldn't break her structured routine at the last minute to give a consequence without front-loading her. If I took TV away, I couldn't say "That's it. No TV for the rest of the day!" or "No dessert today". The change was too sudden for her brain to process and this would escalate into a melt-down which caused dysfunction for days. When discipline was needed, I waited until the next day or days later when she was more put together. I would then tell her that she would lose her TV privileges next Saturday for her behavior last Monday. I read that children with Autism don't lie; they are simply not wired that way. In twenty-five years, I have never, ever known Heather to lie even if it meant telling me she did something that would get her into trouble.

Each time we did a sensory support, it seemed that a layer of fog was lifted and she was a little clearer, calmer, and more like our Heather. Some days the vacancy in her eyes faded, not completely away, but faded. I hadn't dreamt about what Functioning Recovery would look like for Heather. I was too busy struggling to get Heather through the current day and to keep her in as calm a state as possible. Quite honestly, I was just beginning to see glimmers that Functioning Recovery was a possibility.

> *Learning can only happen when a child is interested. If he is not, it's like throwing marshmallows at his head and calling it eating.*
>
> *– Anonymous*

CHAPTER 4

Medical vs. Educational Supports
Get Ready for a Bumpy Ride

Every child with Autism has Sensory Processing Disorder (SPD) but not every child with Sensory Processing Disorder has Autism.

– Dr. Stanley Greenspan

Let's Get the Help We Need

I'M NOT GOING to beat around the bush! The educational system, the way it is designed right now, is broken. It allows the school district to make decisions on medical aspects that they are not qualified to do. There are OT's (Occupational Therapists), PT's (Physical Therapists), and SLP's (Speech and Language Pathologists) who are all medically licensed by your state to uphold all medical criteria for the health and well-being of a child. Those OT's, PT's, SLP's employed by the educational domain view and do their evaluations from a skewed perspective. They only look at the educational performance regardless of the medical impact it may have on a child. If the child is bright and passes the testing administered in the educational domain, as is common for most of the children with High-Functioning Autism, then they do not qualify for any supports. The failure to provide the appropriate accommodating supports in the school environment even if the child passes the testing, hurts that child medically. Heather is a good example of this. Her medical issues escalated in a direct correlation to the increased demands put on her in a school with no access to supports. In Elementary School, the environment is very supportive with few teachers or classroom changes. Heather's Elementary School had approximately 400 students and approximately 600 students in her Middle School compared to her High School with 2,000 students; 7 periods a day, each with a different teacher, different classroom rules, and required higher levels of analytical thinking.

Here is Tip #5: Make sure you, as the parent, understand that as your child enters Middle School and/or High School their supports need to be increased. It is common amongst children with Autism that supports need to be increased in the upper grades due to higher-levels of analytical thinking which are required.

Here are examples of what it was like educationally for Heather: I discussed earlier how in Second Grade she could read Hebrew but couldn't read English. In Third Grade, I noticed a difference in teaching styles. She had a teacher in an environment that shut her down. She couldn't function or show the intellect she had. With the right teacher in the right environment with the right teaching style, Heather would absolutely thrive. With the wrong teacher in the wrong environment, Heather looked like a very different child. I referred her for a 504 *(For a definition of 504 refer to Appendix C)* but was denied even though we'd had an Attention Deficit Disorder (ADD) diagnosis from our regular Pediatrician. Heather started to break down in Second Grade and each year it became more and more difficult to get her to function. The mornings became a perpetual challenge to get Heather out of bed, dressed, and fed before school. Tardiness became a regular event. My husband and I tried and implemented many different consequences for Heather's actions but nothing got through to her. In the Third Grade, Heather had to learn the multiplication tables. At this point, she was a whiz at Math and loved it but couldn't master the tables. When I was this age, I had to write the tables down on paper. I suggested that Heather try this. Writing was a chore for her; she said it hurt her. I called my friends, the educators, in New Jersey. They suggested singing the multiplication tables. Heather went from being behind, enough for the teacher to call me, to learning them all ahead of the class so fast that it prompted the teacher to call me again.

Heather got lice in Fourth Grade. Where I come from, out East, if a child gets gnats on their head or little lice eggs, they're sent home. In my current county, unless they see them alive and crawling around, they leave the child in school. Heather was, repeatedly, getting lice. The situation was rampant through the school. We treated the lice with Rid and some over-the-counter product. This was done twice. The third time, I called the doctor. He prescribed something which we used but Heather got lice again. The chemicals prescribed by the doctor were leaving chemical burns on her head. He told us we could no longer treat Heather. We had to remove her from school for the last month of the school year because they couldn't get rid of the lice problem. I couldn't risk Heather getting lice again with no way to treat it.

In 1996, Heather was nine years old. I spoke to our Pediatrician again. He referred us to Dr. Mann, an Educational Psychologist at Mercy Options, who did a wonderfully thorough evaluation. Heather received her second diagnosis of ADD/ADHD. He made a list of recommendations, which I didn't fully understand at the time but I brought them to the school. In the meantime, the School claimed to see no odd behaviors even though other students were continually teasing Heather about her tic. The tic was evolving; it went from what looked like a shutter to a full-body, hand-wringing, head-tilted, head-rocking episode.

We were trying a series of pharmaceutical drugs for the Attention Deficit. I was concerned that those drugs were hurting her because she was losing so much weight. So, we took her off the drugs and tried some all-natural supports. The Principal was informed of this and I asked him to let the regular teacher know in case he observed any odd behaviors in the classroom. A couple of weeks later, I got a call from the teacher who asked, "What's going on with Heather?" Her ability to focus had deteriorated. When the teacher was in the middle of teaching, Heather would open her desk to dig through it. The inside of her desk looked like a trash can where everything had been dumped. She sang to herself and rocked on her chair. Where the teacher was seeing decline, we were seeing tremendous improvement in how she was at home. She could be touched and she didn't seem nearly as anxious. I asked a lot of questions. I needed to find a way to address her school behaviors. Because of this need, we decided to put her back on some pharmaceutical drugs. It was also because of this behavior escalation that we sought more information in ways to help Heather cope at school and at home. With Dr. Mann's report in hand, I met with the School Psychologist who agreed that a 504 plan would be helpful. I gave the doctor's recommendations to him; he seemed to know and understand what was needed. I would learn years later that some of the recommendations were not inplemented by the school.

During Heather's Fourth and Fifth Grade years, her tic evolved. It went from a slight little shutter to a full-blown shaking, hands-grabbing, twitching behavior at school. We discovered later, while working with psychologists, Heather's brain would literally short-circuit. She would have to trace a number or a letter in her head before she could move forward. This made her more anxious which made the tic more prevalent. It was a vicious cycle. Tardiness and absenteeism became a continual battle at home and with School personal. I frequently commented, "Believe me! If I could get her to school every day on time I would but she doesn't function like others." Homework became a nightmare. Heather was so fatigued at the end of the day that she couldn't keep her eyes open. Homework became a battle.

How was she getting the grades in school if she was having so much trouble doing the work at home? Heather was referred to the school for supports and we had our first 504 meeting to establish services on January 21, 1998. A neurologist had evaluated Heather's tic and I took the information to the school. The 504 suggested that the teachers should seat Heather in front of the class and check in with her if they felt the need to verify that she was paying attention. The report mentioned the tic but it was more in the context that 'Mom says she sees a full body tic at home'. According to the school, Heather exhibited no signs of the tic or other issues while at school.

There were a lot of socialization and behavioral issues starting at this point which is why we started taking her to regular sessions with mental health providers. We hoped to work through some of what was going on and to figure out how to help her. Up to this point, we were not as concerned educationally as we were socially, behaviorally, and medically but clearly those issues were affecting her ability to be educated.

When she transitioned between Fifth and Sixth Grade, she had a class called Tech Ed. A band-saw is used in this class. According to Heather's friends, while waiting in line to use the band-saw, she was experiencing frequent tics. The tic would escalate in frequency and intensity the greater the anxiety. Heather cut off the tip of her finger using the band saw. Imagine a mother's worst phone call. I was told that Heather was in the attendance office with her finger bleeding profusely and that she needed to go to the hospital. Luckily, my son could get to her faster than I could so he took her to the hospital. I met them there. Here's how important it was to have the appropriate and accurate paperwork. Common sense would tell you not to let a child with a full-blown uncontrollable tic use a band-saw but it wasn't in her paperwork. I submitted the Doctor's findings regarding Heather's tic to the school in her Fifth Grade year. It was **not** in the paperwork at the school in her Sixth Grade year. The information didn't transition with her from Elementary School to Middle School. I learned that the child's individual school paperwork, which is what the teachers read, did not necessarily have any medical information on it. Medical information was in the paperwork at the downtown services office. If the 504 paperwork that the teacher read did not specifically say what the child could or couldn't do, that teacher had to provide the same opportunities in the same enviroment as the other students. Hence, a child with a full-body uncontrollable tic is made to use a band-saw that takes precision to operate. I asked the downtown educational office for copies of Heather's records which is how I discovered how the paperwork is manipulated. I found that it **did** appear in the Fifth Grade paperwork but somehow over the summer it disappeared prior to the start of Sixth Grade. I wasn't sure if any of the teachers had current accurate information regarding Heather. How can a teacher teach a child if they are not aware of that child's medical information? Now, I was asking more questions about the school.

I continued to have 504 meetings with the school on June 2, 1998, October 6, 1998, September 15, 1999, and October 3, 2000. I continually tried to show them how Heather was functioning differently and they tried to show me she wasn't. In the 504 paperwork, they added that if the teacher felt it necessary, Heather's instructions should be broken down into simpler steps. It left all the onus of responsibility on the teacher if they felt that Heather needed it.

It was during this time, while working with new mental health providers, that Asperger's Syndrome, High-Functioning Autism, was diagnosed. Of course, I started looking at educational supports for a child with Asperger's. I referred Heather for Special Education on November 28, 2000 under Autism and OHI (Other Health Impaired). [Other Health Impaired means having limited strength, vitality or alertness, due to chronic or acute health problems which adversely affects a child's educational performance.] That became quite the process! I learned through this experience that OT's, PT's, and SLP's who are employed by a school district can't diagnose. They draw their conclusions only based on the educational aspect. They cannot draw unbiased conclusions when they only look at the educational aspect and not at how the process of education affected the child. Basically, if the child is bright and passes the educational version of testing, no support is provided and no information regarding the child's disability is provided to the teachers.

I briefly want to discuss testing: The medical domain recommends that any evaluations being administered are done in their entirety because it gives a good well-rounded view of the child's abilities and deficit areas. The educational domain does a smattering of tests. They cannot diagnose so how do they draw conclusions? Here's an example: I attended an IEP (Individual Educational Plan) for a sixteen year old who was previously identified as qualifying for Special Education. The parent agreed to test as long as the testing was done in its entirety. Not only did a member of the IEP team, the School Psychologist, **not** comply but none of the testing done by anyone in the school drew clear conclusions. The school could have made an argument either way concerning this child's qualifications for Special Education. Luckily, her parents were well informed, had their own independent testing done, and came armed with thorough, accurate information. In the school paperwork, the School Psychologist documented her inability to administer thorough testing because "the mom was uncooperative". How can comments like those **not** perpetuate animosity between the parent and the teacher? The school controls the paperwork so a parent has little power to change what is written.

I had just started reading about Sensory Processing and was looking for an OT which we didn't have. I read The Out of Sync Child *(referred to in Chapter Three)*. I brought that book to Heather's Pediatrician who read it.

By this time, we were back with our original pediatrician (Pediatrician "A") from Medical Facility "A" when we first moved to Wisconsin. He was so moved by what he read that he did two things: 1. He gave Heather a medical excuse for Gym Class. He felt she had a sensory processing issue that needed further evaluation as mentioned previously and also felt that any unnecessary stress impacted Heather medically. 2. He tried to help us find someone who could evaluate Heather for Sensory Processing Disorder. In the meantime, I referred Heather for an evaluation with the School District's OT who agreed and told me she observed some sensory processing differences. It was quietly suggested that I get a second opinion. I couldn't get a second opinion. I was turned away from every OT in the county in which I lived. When OT facilities heard that Heather was almost thirteen years old with a new diagnosis of Asperger's they assumed I must be in a confrontation with the school district so they wouldn't evaluate her. Our search started for an OT. We were turned away from various Madison and Milwaukee facilities until we found Special Therapies, Inc.

Heather was also drowning educationally at this time. Her grades were suffering because of her absences and tardiness. By Seventh Grade, Heather could not do Math in class and was seeing her Math Teacher every day after school so she wouldn't fail. Writing seemed to become an issue. She spoke at a level beyond her years but couldn't seem to write at the same level. The difference between 'talking Heather' and 'written words by Heather' looked like two different people and the penmanship was all over the place; not even on the line. I tried to figure out what to do as the school was telling me that they saw none of what I saw. Interestingly, their written forms stated, "Mom says..." and not that Heather actually had a diagnosis.

I started to question how she was earning the grades they were giving. I was fighting and struggling with Heather all the time about school. Our home life was difficult to say the least. I was fighting to get her up and to school and to get her to address her homework. She was clearly deteriorating. In Seventh Grade, I called a 504 meeting and gave the school a report by Dr. Tony Attwood which recommends that "a child with Asperger's not have homework". It takes so much energy for a child with Asperger's to act 'normal' during the school day that they have nothing left to give to their homework at night. I requested that they stop giving Heather homework. She wasn't watching TV or out playing with friends after school, she was in a melt-down state and unable to function. The school wasn't forth-coming with recommendations or supports so I started to ask for these kinds of supports to ease Heather's stress levels and to try to give her body a chance to rest and rebound in order to do it all over again the next day. Everything was a fight.

> *Autists are the ultimate square peg and the problem with pounding a square peg into a round hole is not that the hammering is hard work; it's that you're destroying the peg.*
>
> *– Paul Collins*

I also started to question the school because Heather was beginning to panic; afraid she was failing. I went to the school to get copies of her work. A teacher was in the midst of copying them when the Principal came in and said that I could not have them. When Heather left Eighth Grade, the teachers and Heather put together a folder as a reflection of her work in Middle School. The work examples provided contradicted what was being said at the meetings. It was filled with examples of Heather presenting her disability at school. This information was in that folder: Heather got a "B" in Social Studies but was failing tests; a reflection sheet attached to a test which she failed showed Heather's concern for her grades. The students were asked to 1. Explain why they did poorly and what they could do differently to improve next time. 2. I chose this piece of work because? Heather answered, "It shows that I need help that I'm not getting." 3. The main thing I learned from this situation? Heather answered, "That I needed more help." 4. If I had it to do all over again? Heather answered," I would try to understand it better." *(Refer to pages 58 and 59 for the Social Studies help sheet images.)*

Heather could not grasp the material with the teaching style which was being used. She simply could not learn in that manner. Clearly no one at school was seeing this. Were they ignoring my concerns? I was baffled. There were other things that were also very frustrating. For example: My niece was on vacation and visiting us. Even though she was a year and a half older, they allowed her to go to school and spend the day with Heather. I had instructed the girls to meet me in front of the school for pick-up at the end of the day. When they weren't there, I parked the car and went in. My niece was sitting in the office and said "Oh, we thought you were in the meeting and were just waiting for you to come out." I went to the Guidance Office and asked them to explain. I was told that the person in charge of 504 for the District had called a meeting. The school had apparently revised the 504 and the Coordinator told the teachers that a parent signature was not required. It was quite a surprise when two days later, April 23, 2001, I got a letter in the mail from the 504 Coordinator informing me that my signature was indeed required and I was to sign the bottom of the enclosed revised 504 into which I had no input. I can't tell you what was going on in this District. I was under the impression people were in this profession to help children but here it seems to be the opposite.

I never saw that 504 Coordinator again; he resigned. Afterwards I went in to meet the new Coordinator. With me, I brought a printed copy from the government website about allowable 504 Services. Keep in mind this was before smartphones and most homes did not have computers. She was surprised by the copy. I asked about her experience. She nicely informed me that she had years of educational experience but no experience in 504. I never saw that woman again. After that, I worked with the Coordinator of Special Education or the Director of Student Services. In 2001, we had 504 meetings on September 12th, 17th and 25th, October 3rd, 30th, November 9th, and December 3rd and 13th. We also had IEP meetings August 30th and September 4th but Heather did not qualify for Special Education. The meetings continued because we couldn't agree on supports.

[Social Studies Self-Assessment]

Name _Heather Goldstein_

Hour _?_   _5-9-01_

SOCIAL STUDIES REFLECTION

CATEGORY OF WORK:

___ Goal Setting   ___ Critical Thinking

___ Performance   ___ Problem Solving

___ Collaboration   _X_ Real Life Application of Knowledge

___ Communication

1. I chose this piece of work because . . . (it shows)

It shows that I need help that I'm not getting.

2. What type of assignment was it? (project, (test,) quiz, homework, etc.)

3. The main thing I learned from this was . . .

that I need more help.

4. If I had it to do over again . . . (How would you improve it?)

I would try to understand it better

[Social Studies Self-Assessment]

Name _Heather Cadwsen_

Hour _2_   _5-9-01_

SOCIAL STUDIES REFLECTION

CATEGORY OF WORK:

___ Goal Setting   X Critical Thinking

___ Performance   ___ Problem Solving

___ Collaboration   ___ Real Life Application of Knowledge

___ Communication

1. I chose this piece of work because . . . (It shows)

    how bad I did

2. What type of assignment was it? (project, test, quiz, homework, etc.)

3. The main thing I learned from this was . . .

    I did bad.

4. If I had it to do over again . . . (How would you improve it?)

    I would read more.

I will remember forever the first meeting in which I met the Coordinator of Special Education. We were in Heather's Middle School. I was trying to explain her full body tic and the anxiety component. As a mother, I really wanted to make sure that she and the school understood the severity of Heather's health picture. I reached out and touched the Coordinator on the arm and I had the most overwhelming and powerful maternal response I'd ever had. I actually pulled my hand away from her; I felt like I'd been burned. I instantly did not trust her. My 'mother-bear' instinct went on heightened alert; something wasn't right. I had never had a response like that. I started to watch her body language and noticed she couldn't make eye contact with me. At one point I finally said to her, "If you're looking for the clock, it's over my right shoulder and not my left shoulder". She wouldn't look at me. It became easy for me to know when I was receiving truthful information based on this woman's body language. It actually helped me along the way but for all the wrong reasons.

Here's an example of the difference between 504 accommodations and Special Education with an IEP and why it was so important with Heather's health issues that she qualified for Special Education: All 504 accommodations are overseen by the School District. If they are not following the 504 plan or you don't agree with it, the same School District that wrote the plan gets to police itself and decide if it's appropriate or not. Do you really think a School District would ever say they were wrong? An IEP for Special Education is overseen by your state's Department of Public Instruction. Parents have recourse if the school is not following the Plan. A complaint can be filed with The Department of Public Instruction at the state level. Your District does not police itself. An IEP also opens the door for your child to receive life skills training and additional educational service until the age of twenty-one. Children with disabilities need these supports to help them live and function independently. Every child, by law, is entitled to FAPE (Free and Appropriate Public Education). This is an educational right for children with disabilities in the U.S. which is guaranteed under the Rehabilitation Act of 1973 and the IDEA Act. Under IDEA, FAPE is defined as an educational program that is individualized to a specific child, designed to meet that child's unique needs, provides access to the general curriculum, meets the grade level standards established by the state and from which the child receives educational benefits. The school under FAPE must provide students with an education including specialized instruction and related services that prepare that child for further education, employment and independent living.

The district tried to appease me. They brought in an Autism Specialist from the Department of Public Instruction (DPI). She was going to help us understand the IEP process. This is when I learned how the educational differs from the medical. Here's another example: Special Education, as the government defines it, 'talks' in grade equivalents when looking at the language written for Special Education. By the government definition of Special Education, if the student is two grade equivalents behind in the learned subjects, Reading, Writing, Spelling, and Math, they qualify for services. There are different categories such as Autism, OHI (Other Health Impaired), LD (Learning Disability), and EBD (Emotionally Behaviorally Disabled) to name a few. The state of Wisconsin doesn't recognize grade equivalents. They work on a 1-100 bell curve. They recognize 16% to 84% as average. In order to qualify, a child must be 4% or below; in other words, practically non-verbal and illiterate. Children on the Autism Spectrum tend to have wide gaps in their raw scores. Apparently, the state law ignores this and doesn't recognize these gaps as adversely affecting education.

This is how that pertained to Heather. She was in Eighth Grade when testing was done. She had verbal skills of a Tenth Grader and written skills of a Fifth Grader. She was three to four grade equivalents behind. Imagine that gap! She spoke like a college professor but wrote like a grammar school kid. How does that child build on educational demands? How was she going to be able to write reports in High School?

Additional independent testing done outside of the school showed that Heather had what is called Non-Verbal Problem Solving Ability. This was a big issue for her in Math. No wonder she was spending every day after school with her Math Teacher in Middle School. When she was given a problem, she was able to give the answer but not able to break down the steps to show how she got the answer. She couldn't put it in writing or speak it. In High School, they implied that Heather was getting her answers from other sources. I suggested that they let Heather go into a room by herself to do her work. They refused. The problem: If she didn't get the correct answer, they didn't know how to help her because they couldn't see her work and she couldn't tell them.

In the sequence of events, Heather was now in the IEP process for eligibility. We went through an arduous process of school-version testing. The school has no obligation to accept or use independent testing nor required to use current testing material. How accurate and up-to-date are their evaluations? My School District used testing materials that were no longer recognized in the medical domain as appropriate as a stand-alone diagnosis for Asperger's Syndrome. During the eligibility meeting, I was trying to explain Heather's production of life-threatening levels of stress hormones based on my conversations with the Endocrinologist. The School Nurse, by her own admission, had very little training in Endocrinology but she continued to tell the IEP Team that it was not a cause for concern. In the IEP meeting, the IEP team found Heather to be ineligible for Special Education while my input as a parent was disregarded. Now, what do we do? Something is not right! The school is not forthcoming with information and Heather is clearly breaking down.

I was learning new and potentially helpful information every day. I also had scheduled Heather for some independent testing. This was the only way we were getting information about Heather's functioning. I had even thought about consulting an attorney as I continued to get a handle on educational supports. I was networking with private Autism Consultants in Madison. I had acquired the name of a new Educational Psychologist in Madison who specialized in Autism Spectrum Disorders. She was quickly becoming an expert and advocate in the field. She asked, "What kind of evaluations does the school administer?" I explained my information and described how Heather functioned before, during, and after school and in different surroundings. I was told that Heather needed an evaluation that showed her ability to function across environments. This advocate was so concerned about the type of testing that was done; she met me at a restaurant near Interstate-90 in order to give me the proof that the school's testing was inadequate. She gave me a report from the Journal of Autism and Developmental Disorders, Vol. 29. No. 2, 1999 titled, <u>A Screening Questionnaire for Asperger Syndrome and Other High-Functioning Autism Spectrum Disorders in School Age Children.</u>

When Heather was denied for Special Education eligibility the first time, I initially filed for a Due Process hearing but rescinded prior to the investigation. Heather was getting independent testing and I was taking a Wrights law course on Special Education. I also started working with CESA 2 (Central Education Service Area 2), The Wisconsin Coalition of Advocacy, and Wisconsin Facets. Wisconsin Coalition of Advocacy and Wisconsin Facets are both statewide grant-funded advocacy groups. Their goal is to help parents advocate for educational services for their children. Both, as does CESA 2, have people that specialize in Autism. I was being told different things by these organizations versus the school. I learned that the state prefers to see that all the steps have been attempted; Independent Educational Evaluation and Mediation, prior to going to Due Process. I wasn't sure who to trust but these individuals understood what I was telling them. With their experience, they were giving sound advice. I trusted them more than our school district. I was already working with two state recognized Independent Educational Evaluators so I opted for the Mediation step.

The school's actions made me feel unable to trust any school district personal. Every person that the school recommended as having expertise in Autism and was supposed to be unbiased was not. That was a big contention for me. If I move forward with Mediation, will that person really be impartial? I had recently learned that the School District's Parent Liaison and the Autism Specialist which the school brought in, were in fact paid employees of the School District. The Parent Liaison who offered to take notes for me was unable to provide those notes after the meeting because she was paid by the school. The Autism Consultant was not a representative from the Department of Public Instruction as she was introduced to me. How was either of these people unbiased? The school's actions continued to perpetuate a feeling of distrust between us and them.

I was trying to help other parents. I was learning a lot and advocating for a particular family. Their child also had Autism but was younger than Heather. In a meeting with the administrator, I, again, had that maternal 'mother-bear' response that I wasn't getting all of the information. She was the LEA (Lead Educational Advisor) on the IEP Team. During a meeting, we were discussing the benefits for this child and what supports would be available since the present supports were not working. This child was exhibiting language skill problems. He had a vocabulary of three hundred words at home compared to six at school. We were told by the LEA that if the mother took her child out of public school in favor of home-school, he would continue to receive the same supports he currently had. We ended the meeting; the mom wanted the opportunity to speak to her husband. We decided to reconvene the following week with a yes or no answer. When we met again, we were told that the LEA had never said that the child would get the same supports. We ended the meeting and filed a complaint with the Department of Public Instruction. The District sends paperwork to the DPI and a decision is made whether or not this information was in compliance. This mother called me and was very upset because the paperwork sent to the DPI reported that at no time did the LEA say that the child would receive the same supports if he was home-schooled. The mother had mentioned that the paid School Parent Liaison was at the meeting. The DPI had no record of it so it was the school's word against hers. I was asked to write a letter which I did. Not only did the LEA say that this child would get the same benefits if he was home-schooled but the Parent Liaison heard it; I knew this because she was sitting next to me. That woman did do many things for so many families within the confines allowed but she was an employee of the District. She was not unbiased. When we, as parents, wanted factual information about our children, we wanted it to come from unprejudiced support. DPI found in favor of the mom.

As I was preparing for Mediation, scheduled for May of 2001, I received a lot of good information from the Middle School packet put together by Heather and her teachers. Included were great examples of how Heather exhibited her inability to apply the information she was learning. For example: In her written Math work, she referred to cars being 30 feet long; a woman's shoe box being 6 feet; a table being 13 inches off the ground. This was typical, I would learn, for children with Autism. They have trouble applying or exhibiting what they learn in their lives. The most surprising and profound information came from the Terra Nova test results in Fourth Grade and Eighth Grade. Terra Nova is a mandated, state-wide test administered in these two grade levels. Under the Knowledge and Concepts Exam in Fourth Grade, Heather was Proficient to Advanced across the board with the highest scores in Math. The Writing Report gives a Holistic score: 1 being the lowest and 6 being the highest. Heather scored a 4. The exam states for a score of 4: Response is completely organized and developed; adequate use of language and mechanics. See diagram below.

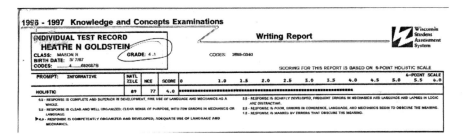

In Eighth Grade, Heather's Math scores had fallen to a Basic Level. Her Writing Holistic score had fallen to 2.5: Response is poor, errors in coherence, language and mechanics begin to obscure meaning; response is scantily developed, frequent errors in mechanics and language and lapses in logic are distracting. See diagram below.

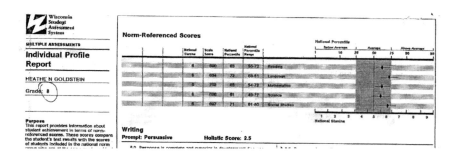

I thought for sure the school could explain and address the changes in the scores. I didn't know what to think about the language but I was noticing Heather was missing parts of conversations or couldn't, in heightened states of anxiety, tell me a story coherently. It was sequentially out of order. This is when I started to ask the Who-What-Where-When-How-and-Why questions. I needed to understand what she was telling me.

Through a conversation with the Mediator, I learned that she was knowledgeable and willing to help. Her job was to resolve the conflict. Here is how the mediation worked: An unbiased person from Marquette University came to our district. In the Mediation meeting was the Mediator, Stan and me, the Director of Student Services, the District-paid Autism Specialist, the Coordinator of Student Services and the School's OT. First, the Mediator asked if the Director of Student Services had decision-making power on behalf of the District for Mediation. She assured us that she did. I was hopeful for some resolutions. I came prepared with a demonstration including visuals of Heather's disability. I talked about the books on Asperger's and Heather's characteristics. I discussed the Sensory Processing Disorder component. I brought up the Doctor's excuse from Gym Class. I brought the information from the medical team who was working with Heather who were recommending a modified school day because of her "life-threatening levels of ACTH adrenal stress hormones". This was an arduous meeting that lasted for hours in a hot room while I presented Heather's case: I discussed her tardiness, absentee-ism, and her escalations; her reduced ability to sustain in certain environments, how literal she was, her need for routines and rituals which is all typical for a child with Autism. I brought in books which discussed the ASD and the SPD characteristics. They had the same books in the Special Education office. I also shared our independent evaluations with them. I pleaded my case for supports. I tried to talk about her issues with the pragmatics of speech but we wouldn't have an independent speech evaluation until September. I showed the Terra Nova scores as another example of Heather's educational impact. In their eyes, Heather was suffering educationally because of tardiness and absenteeism because I was taking her out of school during school hours for therapy. Mediation was not a pleasant task. After four hours of getting nowhere, the Mediator asked the Director of Student Services if she still had decision-making power for the District and we were told 'no'. The Director of Student Services explained that her attorney, not at the meeting but in the room next door advising the district during the entire time, suggested that the IEP Team needed to reconvene with the new information which was just presented and then they would vote. How naive I was. I thought we'd sit down, hash it out, and move forward. Mediation is designed as a step before consulting an attorney but the district was consulting their attorney during the entire time. We had to get an attorney! The Mediator left it up to us. She felt that we did a good job presenting Heather's information so it would not be a bad thing to reconvene the IEP. The IEP did reconvene, the new information was presented, and Heather was found **not** eligible for Special Education. We retained an attorney.

In mid-September of 2001, the beginning of her Ninth Grade year, Heather was evaluated by an SLP at the UW Hospital. It was too late to include this information in the IEP eligibility meeting but we would have it for the 504 Plan. The specifics and details of independent evaluations gave us clearer, more detailed and accurate information regarding Heather's abilities and inabilities. For Speech and Language, the pathologist looked at expressive language (how well one speaks) and at receptive language (how well a person comprehends when addressed). In children with Low-Functioning Autism, like Pervasive Developmental Disorder, a child could be non-verbal. Most children with Asperger's speak but they have a problem with the pragmatics or the use of speech. Heather had a problem in this area but more so in writing than speaking. In writing, she showed a grade equivalent of a Fifth Grader. She was found to have problems in syntax, spelling, and style of writing. She was in the 99% for vocabulary, 30% in problem solving, 42% in linguistics, 37% in language composition and ambiguous sentences, and 25% in inferences and recreating sentences. How was she going to be able to keep up with the writing demands in High School?

One thing that bothered me about the testing was that the evaluator, seeing Heather's age, made comments regarding conflicts between us, Heather's parents, and the school. This evaluator was very clear that she would not get involved in the fight to get services. This was a common response from most independent evaluators in the medical domain. They seemed to understand the medical /educational conflict but no one wanted to reach out to help or explain the conflict.

My pediatrician alone had written twelve letters between December 8th, 2000 and November 27th, 2001. Every letter said the same thing; Heather has Asperger's Syndrome, Sensory Processing Disorder, produces life-threatening levels of stress hormones, has a full body tic, serious severe allergies to food and environment therefore he recommends a modified school day and a medical excuse for Gym Class. The Endocrinologist, the Neurologist, the OT, and the Mental Health Provider all recommended this. The school refused every time. This is when I learned to not let the school have open communication with our doctor. For example: The doctor and I would have a discussion and he then would write a letter based on that discussion. The school would then call the doctor right before a meeting and ask questions. The school personal would then say that the doctor never said that or he did not write his recommendations correctly. After twelve letters and much frustration on the doctor's part, he finally refused to write anymore letters to the school. It was a semantics game to the Director of Student Services. She would ask the doctor, "What is the medical protocol if Heather seems to fatigue easily?" His response was," You can try modifying her school day". The district said that the doctor wrote it wrong; they did not have to follow it and threatened Truancy Detention if Heather did not attend. I did 2 things: I called the head of Juvenile Detention. I had heard from other parents that truancy came with a stay in the Detention Center and a fine that prevents a student from getting their diploma unless the fines are covered. I met with the head of Juvenile Detention. I told him Heather's story and showed him copies of the medical recommendation. He didn't see how he could ever come after Heather for truancy based on the documentation shown to him. He assured me that I didn't need to be concerned. The school was very surprised when I told them I had resolved any truancy issues concerning Juvenile Detention. I also called the office of Civil Rights and explained Heather's situation. They gave excellent advice which was to get the school policy for absenteeism.

It was a very good day to go to the District Office. While I was waiting for the policy, I walked into the Special Education Office. There were book shelves filled with books and supports. I looked through them and wrote down the titles. Some, I had already read such as <u>Asperger's Syndrome, A Guide for Parents and</u> <u>Professionals</u> by Tony Attwood, <u>The Out of Sync Child</u> , <u>Sensory Supports within</u> <u>a Classroom</u> both by Carol Stock Kranowitz, but <u>Asperger's Syndrome and Adolescence : Practical Solutions For School Success</u> by Brenda Smith-Myles was new.

I purchased the book and read it. I even attended the author's seminars and reached out to them to consult with me regarding Heather. Now, I had information to use when making requests for school supports. When I spoke to my pediatrician about reducing Heather's stress by modifying her school day, I would make references to certain authors and cite what their book(s) suggested. When I attended that Autism conference with Brenda Smith-Myles, Heather's entire Support Team from school was in the back of the room. I was in the midst of trying to get the school to modify her school day. I was in the front row of the conference and raised my hand. I explained that my daughter had life-threatening levels of stress hormones; she had Asperger's and Sensory Processing Dysfunction. Would asking the school to modify her day be an appropriate intervention? This speaker couldn't have agreed more that this needed to be done. I thought that maybe this would get us somewhere because many of the key players in the IEP Team were at this conference. If they were hearing what I was hearing, they surely would agree. Sadly, this was not to be the case. By the time the school finished quizzing Heather's pediatrician about medical protocol (the recognized pediatrician for the school district) he didn't want to write any more letters. He said he would do whatever he could to help Heather but he wasn't going to deal with the school. He was the third doctor who informed me that there would be no further dealings with the school. The school refused to modify Heather's schedule.

Here's the semantics game: In the medical domain, a doctor writes a recommendation or a protocol to follow. The educational domain does not recognize these words as required for education. What I learned from getting the School Board Policy on absenteeism, though, was that the school recognizes a medical excuse. My doctor wrote one more letter. It gave Heather a medical excuse from school from 8:00 am until 11:30 am every day for the same reasons he had addressed in previous letters. The school had no choice but to honor it.

Another thing to keep in mind: My husband and I were paying thousands and thousands of dollars per year to get the best support for Heather. It is estimated that the average cost per year for supports for a child with Autism is $15,000 to $20,000. We could not have this undermined by a group of teachers unqualified in Autism and Sensory Processing Disorders. I told the District that if they wanted any information, it must be submitted in writing to me then I would get an answer for them in writing. They no longer got open communications with anyone from my medical team. I had to protect the people who were helping us and still function through this crazy school system.

As luck would have it, I was very vocal at school board meetings and asked questions about the process. A lot of parents reached out to me. I was stopped at the grocery store or slipped a note with their phone number on it. I called them and listened to their stories and struggles, many of which regarded truancy. That is how I learned to resolve my potential truancy problem. I had been warned by other parents to go directly to juvenile detention.

By this point, Heather was having melt-downs which lasted for five days with no communication. I taught her simple sign language in order to connect with us when she couldn't communicate. This problem was worse in the morning which is why she had a delayed start of school. She was in no condition to be educated. This is when she started having issues with speaking in sequential order.

I knew the School Psychologist was starting to understand Heather's symptoms. She allowed Heather to rest one day at school when she was fatigued and the Psychologist had difficulty waking her. I hoped this awareness was support on Heather's side.

The school environment was negative with contradicting medical recommendations and refusal to provide supports. Everything we eventually received from the school was a long process with many long meetings in an environment that was undesirable. The school complained and documented that I was not allowing or teaching Heather how to advocate for herself. No, we weren't allowing her to advocate at school but we worked together with Heather and her medical providers, the OT, the SLP, the pediatrician, and the social worker to get her input. The medical domain was open, willing to help, and accepting of Heather's needs. In this environment, we talked about education with Heather and what she felt she needed in order to be successful. I brought the information to school to fight for it. The demands of school became so great that we had to make changes to Heather's schedule.

We allowed Heather to enjoy dance until High School when it became clear that she could not maintain school, therapies, and dance. Dance and Music were wonderful supports for her. Her tic was really bad by Middle School. Her Dance Teacher called me a few times because Heather was stuck in her tic so bad back stage before she danced it looked like a mild epileptic seizure. I told her to start the music. It was amazing to see the calming effect it had on Heather. The change was visible as she heard that classical music. Her shoulders dropped, her body relaxed, and she danced. That dance could last 2-6 minutes and you never saw that tic. It disappeared during the dance. I was sorry we couldn't find a way to continue this for Heather but she simply had very little stamina with the demands of Ninth Grade and no appropriate supports.

Here is Tip #6: It is common for children with High-Functioning Autism to excel in Math and Music.

A lot of children with Asperger's are very pedantic or robot-like with their speech. When Heather was younger, we spent a lot of time role-playing to teach behaviors and articulation. We were very animated when we told stories. I felt this would be very beneficial. Here was a good aspect of Ninth Grade. How phenomenal it was to meet a drama teacher who came to us, knowing of Heather's Asperger's, and said, "I noticed Heather is a little stiff in her movements but I think she'd do really well in the play. She can audition?" Theatre was like a therapy with role playing and socialization aspects. I thought this would be a good support in place of Dance Class. The school didn't understand why a child couldn't come to school until after 11:30 am but could stay late and participate in Theater. Her issue was modulation in the morning. This was a child with chronic fatigue trying to make it through a day and doing the best she could. The Drama Teacher had no problem being flexible with Heather's schedule.

A problem with a 504, as I mentioned before, is if the school is not following the plan or includes or excludes things with which you don't agree, the district is doing their own policing. It's an aspect that is very wrong with the system. It is also why I was continually encouraged, by the educational advocate with which I worked, to push for Heather to qualify for Special Education. I'm glad I was vocal about Autism. One of those angel teachers told me to be concerned about High School Chemistry Lab. She explained that the school would require Heather to sign the Flinn's Scientific Student Safety Contract. The contract is designed to make the students responsible and aware of the breakable, combustible materials being used. They would be working with glass containers and Bunsen Burners mixing chemicals to look for reactions. The contract holds the student personally and financially responsible for any breakage or damage. Here's where you have to be proactive with Autism and SPD. My daughter has smell, touch, and anxiety issues. If there is a sudden chemical reaction, she may have a primal response to those reactions and unintentionally drop or throw something. If Heather didn't sign the contract, she would fail the class. I signed for her and added footnotes to the contract noting that the school was aware of her Asperger's and SPD and could not hold Heather accountable if the class triggered a reaction resulting in damage.

Here are some situations that made a difference. Heather was being excused from Gym Class. Her Pediatrician had come and talked to the school staff (with myself present) explaining Heather's "fragile medical condition". Heather had a sustainable 3.5 hour window to keep it together. We felt that this time would be best spent in her academic classes. Another reason for Heather being exempt from Gym Class was her non-understanding of the dynamics in competitive play. She liked to play volleyball but couldn't handle the competitiveness. The environment was too stressful for her when other players picked a weak-link and 'nailed' that person with volleys and spikes. Also, the entire routine of getting undressed, showering, and redressing was all unnecessary sensory input for a child with Autism. She could get credits in other ways like her summer dance classes. So after this meeting with her Pediatrician, her Guidance Counselor pulled Heather out of class and took her into her office. I wasn't there so I only know what happened based on Heather's response and sessions afterwards with her Mental Health Provider. It would take several days before I discovered fully what had happened. This was during Heather's Tenth Grade year.

I dropped Heather off at school the day after the Pediatrician had come to speak about Gym Class and Heather's health condition. I could feel that something was wrong but I couldn't put my finger on it. It scared me. Heather's mental state was tenuous. It seemed as if she'd gone to the edge of insanity where she could have gone either off the 'deep end' or been reeled back to reality. I'd felt this energy before. I followed my instincts, parked the car, and went into the school. I asked the front office to please excuse Heather from class. I was there to remove her from school. They wouldn't release her. I asked why and they said Heather was fine. They asked me to wait in the Principal's Office which I did for twenty minutes. The Principal asked me why I wanted to remove Heather from school. I explained to him that being her mother and understanding her disability, I knew something was not right. I wanted them to remove Heather from class and let me speak to her. I continued to wait. Finally, I saw Heather's Vice-Principal who was part of Heather's Support Team.

Here is Tip #7: If you have a child with Autism, you will need to create a Support Team available to your child within their school. Through my urgings, a Support Team had been added to the 504 plan. The Team consisted of a group of school personal who had attended training in Asperger's, understood Heather's health issues and how Heather presented her Autism, and were available for Heather if she needed them. This was a typical educational support for a child with Autism.

I told the Vice-Principal, "I want to see Heather. Something isn't right." She refused. Yes, the school flat-out refused. I remember telling them that until Heather was eighteen years old, I was responsible for her health and well-being and I wanted to see Heather. They continued to refuse so I called the Police from the Main Office. I spoke quietly as I explained my situation. This was like kidnapping. The regular Police didn't come but they sent the School District's Police Officer who worked at the school to maintain discipline on school grounds. He was sent to the Office to speak with me. I was firmly escorted to an enclosed conference room where I explained that Heather was under the age of eighteen, I was her mother, and I had serious concerns about her. I felt like I was being 'grilled' by this Policeman. I went on to explain about Heather's Asperger's and Sensory Processing Disorder and that I couldn't be specific but I had good instincts and felt that something wasn't right with Heather. Autism is about communication and sometimes it's not about verbal communication. I knew something wasn't right and I needed to see my daughter. The Police Officer asked if I had proof that Heather had a disability. I looked at the Vice-Principal and said that the school has all of that information and that he was free to look at it himself. The Vice-Principal replied that she had none of that information. Really? After all those meetings over the years and the school had nothing to show the Officer that's paid and employed by the District? I said," Until the age of eighteen, I'm responsible for her. I want you to release her or I'm filing a kidnapping charge". The Officer decided that the Vice-Principal would go up and talk to Heather. After some time, she returned and said that Heather told her that she'd hurt herself the night before at home. Heather said she'd poked herself with sewing needles between her toes and though it didn't hurt while she was doing it, it hurt today. The Police Officer wanted to know why Heather was allowed to have needles if she had a disability. I explained that she often used them to sew her ballet shoes.

I was heart-sick to hear this news but I could feel the conflict in Heather. This was a typical Autism conflict. I taught Heather that her job as a child was to listen to her parents, listen to her doctors, and then listen to her teachers. She didn't know who to listen to first; this was her conflict. I also taught her if she was ever in trouble or knew someone in trouble, she should tell a person of authority in order to get help. The Vice-Principal and the Police Officer agreed to release her. My heart ached for Heather. I had to work with this information. I didn't know what to say or where to begin. We drove home in silence as I observed Heather breaking down into a shut- down state. Before I drove the less-than-half mile to our house, I could see Heather dissolve. This is a typical characteristic of Asperger's. Where does a child feel the safest? They feel safest in their homes. It's their comfort zone of unconditional love; unconditional mother's love. No matter how she melted down, she could count on me. It's never changed how I feel or think about her. It scared me to watch her 'dissolve'. She got out of the car, laid down on the cement in the middle of the driveway, and I couldn't get her up. She was crying and hysterical. After some time, I got her inside onto the carpeted family room just inches beyond the entry way. She was in a fetal position and crying. I was trying to understand what she was saying but it didn't make sense to me. I couldn't follow her. I tried my Who-What-When-When-How-and-Why technique but I still couldn't understand. It had to do with Gym Class: being able to take Gym, not tell me, didn't want to lie to me and she didn't want her Guidance Counselor at school to get in trouble. I called her Mental Health Therapist immediately and her Pediatrician. It took a while to get through the whole story. Heather and I talk about it now. She was terribly confused and depressed. She wanted to listen to me and she knew she couldn't lie. She liked volleyball and wanted to take some components of Gym Class. She understood the Guidance Counselor to say that she could take Gym but she just couldn't tell me or the doctor. This conflict was the catalyst for Heather to hurt herself.

Here is Tip #8: Make decisions for your child even if they or the school don't like it or understand it. When you're talking about your child, you might have a difference of opinion with the school; you and your child might have differences of opinions. Sometimes you have to make decisions for your child whether they like it or not. I had to make the decision that Heather couldn't attend Gym Class knowing that she enjoyed aspects of it. I understood the sensory system implications for Heather if she attended this High School class. The doctors and I agreed that a larger class size, more competitive play dynamics, and changing/showering would not be in Heather's best interest. The school didn't understand the implications for Heather so they contradicted us every time they spoke to her.

What the school was not grasping was that Therapies became more important than school because Heather was clearly exhibiting deterioration in her actions. I want to point out: My husband and I made no unilateral decisions concerning Heather. We were working with a pediatrician, an OT, two endocrinologists, a neurologist, a mental health provider, two Autistic Spectrum Disorder advocates, and two educational psychologists that specialized in Autistic Spectrum Disorders. Thus far, my observations from the school were that it was obvious who had no training in Autism, who had school-version-censored-training, and who had independent training.

Here is Tip #9: Do not be afraid to ask school personal, including Art, Music, Gym, cafeteria monitors, and/or library staff, what kind of training they've had in Autism. Anyone who has contact with your child during the school day should have information about your child's Autism. These people should be included in the school meetings.

Heather was learning about her disability and how she functioned. It was like teaching a diabetic about blood sugar. They can eat candy but they may not see the effect right away. If they ignore their disability, at some point, it will drastically impact their health.

What Heather didn't yet understand was we, her parents, and her medical team, were concerned that any unnecessary stimulation would be worse for her. She didn't understand the impact it had on her system. These were "the lost years". She was in and out of a fog-state most of the time but we were doing our best to keep her together. She was torn between listening to us and listening to what she was being told at school. This conflict caused her additional anxiety; the greater the anxiety, the greater the Autistic characteristics. The situation caused her such anxiety and emotional distress that she hurt herself physically so she wouldn't feel the hurt emotionally. It's not much different than the Gate Theory which I learned in CranioSacral Therapy training. These children with neuro-developmental delays bang their heads because the pressure is so intense. The pain of hitting their heads against something redirects the ongoing pain they feel. And that's what it was like for Heather. A terrible thing! We had very clear guidelines in our house against this type of behavior. Heather had tried to hurt herself once before so any further episodes like that would not be tolerated. We immediately took her for additional therapy sessions to address this unacceptable behavior and to figure out why she felt she had to hurt herself. Heather didn't want to lie to us or her doctor or get the Guidance Counselor in trouble. She was afraid to take Gym Class under those conditions which drove her to exhibit that behavior. Getting conflicting information at school undermines the therapy and information she was receiving from her doctors. This was not going to work this way.

Our biggest issue at this point was trying to help Heather develop a Sensory Diet or Lifestyle. We told her to try Sensory Supports in school to reduce her anxiety. The school wouldn't let her do this and told her that she didn't have Autism. We felt that we were never going to get her to where she understands the importance of this therapy unless everyone was on the same page. *Here is Tip #10: When working with a child with Autism, everyone should have the same goals and should be speaking the same language.* We couldn't have been further apart than we were at that time.

It took almost three years to find and start working with an independent OT. We found Sue Kratz who, at the time, was with Developmental Therapies, Inc. in Waukesha. Being an independent therapist, we were paying for her services out of our own pocket and welcomed the opportunity to do so. Ms. Kratz used part of the evaluation which the school had administered but did her own observation work to draw her conclusions. Her evaluation concluded that Heather had 'definite differences' in fourteen different areas with palpable differences in six and typical performance only in three. The areas in which she had definite differences were emotional-social responses, behavioral outcome of sensory processing, modulation of sensory input affecting her emotional responses, and modulation of movement affecting her activity levels. She also had auditory processing problems, oral sensory processing problems, emotional re-activeness, low endurance and tone, oral sensory sensitivity, serious inattentive distracting, and poor resonation, sedentary, and fine motor perceptual. Those were all included in the 'definite differences'. This was a substantially different report than what I received from the school. The school showed or said that Heather only had some sensory differences. Ms. Kratz taught us how to be detectives and figure out how to help Heather adapt to an environment and modulate the behaviors. I have spoken to many different parents in many different states and each parent who has discussed Functioning Recovery has talked about Sensory Processing Disorder. If you adapt the environment for your child then your child can't ever function outside of that adaptive environment. At some point, you have to teach that child tools to self-access because to function independently in the real world, they will have to learn how to self-regulate. They have to have the tools to balance their systems; they have to understand how their system responds in different environments to avoid the erratic behaviors. Some children with Autism have very extreme social behaviors which makes it impossible for them to be in any environment. With Ms. Kratz's help, Heather learned which environments in which she could function, which she needed to avoid, and which she could use self-access supports to function for a period of time. This was still not firmly established but we continued the work since this was our goal with our OT.

Ms. Kratz wrote a very detailed report about Heather's current sensory state; the sensory differences, her recommendations, and suggested a modulation program and how that would be helpful in school. The Modulation Program is designed to learn what can boost a child who is melting/shutting down or how to calm a child who is escalating and develop a sensory diet. The goal is to keep the child balanced in 'the middle'. She suggested the program, How Does Your Engine Run? Heather felt that it was a bit juvenile for

High School age so based on her suggestion, we decided to use faces. Initially, Heather drew only a happy face in the middle, a crazy face for when she was agitated, and a sad face for when she was melting down. Eventually, this evolved to five faces when she began to recognize signs of shutting down or being hyper. We would systematically see, based on tried sensory supports, what would escalate her or what would deescalate her. It worked great at home. We became sensory detectives. To this day, when Heather goes into new environments, we have to problem-solve potential solutions to help her succeed. She needed to modulate on her own by learning some coping mechanisms. That was the lesson we needed to teach her. I felt that it was my job to make the school understand this. I needed their help in order for this to happen.

I know some parents would say that we could have moved or you could have home-schooled. I would have made those choices if it had been in Heather's best interest. It wasn't; the entire medical team agreed. How was she going to adapt in new environments and mature to adulthood when she doesn't leave our house? At this point, her world was a routine of school-home-therapy. How was she going to socialize in the real world? I started looking at options but there weren't any desirable or allowable options. I thought she could get a HSED (High School Equivalency Diploma). She wouldn't have to attend school from 8:00 am to 3:00 pm. The classes were usually held at a local technical college and were three or four hours in duration. A student could work at one's own pace. in our School District, a student must get permission from the school to do this. A student could not opt for this kind of diploma on their own unless the students' graduating class had already graduated and the student had failed to graduate with them. The district refused. What would Heather do for the next two years at home? Locally, there were some private school options but for us, there was an obstacle. The private schools were all parochial schools with Christian-based aspects. These schools would not accept Heather's Jewish religious training as fulfillment for their religious education requirements. There was the Waldorf School in Milwaukee which is supposed to be the best school environment for most children on the Autism Spectrum. The students stay with the same teacher year after year and work in the same kind of structured classroom environment throughout school. Sadly, this was not an option due to the commuting distance.

I saw great declines in Heather every time we moved. She was born in the Houston area in Texas. We moved when she was an infant to Arlington, Texas. When she was three years old, we moved to Virginia and by the age of four, we moved to Abington, Maryland. When Heather was five years old, we moved to BelAir, Maryland and at seven and a half, we moved to Wisconsin. Another move would cause more disruption and anxiety. This left us no choice but to work within the District. Always, our thoughts were in Heather's best interest.

Heather was attending school for 3.5 hours a day. Due to the medical excuse to address absenteeism, the school had no choice but to provide a home-bound instructor. Math was a wise choice given the nonverbal problem solving abilities Heather exhibited. She was **still** melting down from the school environment. It was a task-by-task, function-by-function struggle to keep Heather going which is why we continued to ask the school for help.

Here's Tip #11: Author, Brenda Smith-Myles, recommends having the school assign a one-on-one aide for your child to keep them on-task, organized, and focused. The school did not support this at all. I acted as an aide but from home.

The Home-Bound Instructor was really a nice woman who came at 9:00 am one day per week. The Home-Bound Instructor was not qualified to discuss Heather's disability but she saw her working on the floor because she could not balance her system to sit in a chair. Hence, the delayed start to her school day. One or two days a week

Heather could handle getting up early but she could not sustain that every day. When we tried early and late starts Heather couldn't balance her system; she needed that steady reduced-schedule with a later start. That was her modulation need. Heather was also trying some sensory supports to try to help balance her system in the morning. Heather worked with a knitted afghan pulled tight over her head. She could see to do her work as she gave herself some deep pressure; a calming Sensory Support technique. Heather had trouble modulating her system through these years. Sometimes, she literally could not get up and stand erect. She looked like she was drunk.

One of the reasons our School District had difficulty accommodating a modified school day is that they only offered failure-based summer school. Ideally, the person with Autism could attend school a half a day year round for structure and consistency. In our District, students had to take a class during the school year and fail that class before they would be allowed to be enrolled in a summer school class. Surrounding school districts stopped failure-based summer school years ago and can now better accommodate children on the Autism Spectrum. Our District's summer school students were at-risk students; not a student population that would be appropriate for Heather. We were concerned about Hidden Curriculum as it pertains to Heather or a child with Autism.

Here is one of the best pieces of information I learned about behaviors with children with Autism and how they think. It's called a Hidden Curriculum. If you are watching football and a touchdown is scored, the players head-butt, body-pump, or smack the player who made the successful play. The child with Autism will view this behavior and mimic it in Gym Class. As long as he/she keeps seeing it on national television, this will be perceived as normal behavior. They will have trouble understanding why they are getting consequences for exhibiting the same behavior. This is why putting a child on the Autism Spectrum in a class with children that are emotionally and behaviorally challenged is not appropriate. They should be in a class where they can see examples of neuro-typically normal children function.

Here is Tip #12: When planning activities with your child, beware of the potential for Hidden Curriculum.

Heather was still having five-day-a-week shutdowns. Sometimes it took us hours to arouse her in order to get her to school on time for 11:30 am. This was not because we didn't try the tough love, drag-out-of- bed approach. It simply didn't work and it escalated the situation. As I mentioned in Chapter Two, Heather had no R.E.M. cycle when she was sleeping. She was in bed all that time because it took her body that long to feel like it had achieved a degree of rest. The Neurologist explained that a person's central nervous system doesn't calm down until it has that R.E.M. state to promote rest and relaxation in the body.

Heather was entering her junior year. At this rate, she would not graduate with her class. It was a constant, continual struggle. Based on all the current independent evaluations on Heather, the advice of Wisconsin Facets, and the Educational Psychologists, I referred Heather for Special Education, again, and requested an IEP eligibility meeting. My key school consultants for the Autism supports at this time were Jan Serak, the Director for WI Facets in Milwaukee, and the Educational Psychologist in Madison who specialized in Autism Spectrum Disorders. Along with my request for Special Education, I asked the ADOS (Autism Diagnostic Observation Schedule) Evaluation be administered. According to my Educational Consultant, it was the best evaluation available. It allowed the evaluator to observe the child across environments. That made perfect sense to me because Heather's OT and I thought we were seeing that the supports Heather needed in Math differed from the supports she needed in English or Science.

The school paperwork for the 504 Plan stated that teachers could allow for sensory breaks. Great! What does that mean? What are you doing that constitutes a sensory break? They couldn't answer my question. At home, Heather would use proprioception or deep pressure to her body. She bounced on a big yoga ball for deep pressure. If she was over-stimulated or too anxious, she would go to a quieter room, maybe where the lights were dimmer, where she would isolate herself from others. We needed to help her find appropriate supports which were acceptable to self-administer at school. We needed to know her obstacles and choices to help the situation. She couldn't, for example, go into the cafeteria in the school. It was too loud. It was too uncomfortable for her. It threw off her system. In the younger grades, she would lean in on other people so she would feel grounded but this was not an acceptable choice in High School. We found a quiet spot in the Guidance Office which is where she went. The ADOS Evaluation would help us assemble that information in school.

I was always conscientious of the District's financial concerns. With any suggestion I made, I offered to pay. With any suggestions they had that they felt would help, I offered to pay but they declined. I offered to volunteer forty hours a week to the district if they would help us to help Heather. I just wanted to help my daughter in any way that I could. I was called to a meeting at the administration office. I met the Director of Student Services and the Coordinator of Special Education. They had the referral letter which I had written to request Special Education for Heather. It included my request for the ADOS Evaluation to be utilized. They told me that it was off the market and was no longer being used. I laughed and excused myself in order to call the advocate in Madison to verify that information but couldn't get through to her. I told them that I could not believe they thought I would believe them just because they said it. They implied that I was delaying the IEP process. I ended the meeting, walked out, and got in touch with the Educational Psychologist Advocate. I asked if the ADOS Evaluation was off the market because that was what the school had told me. She could not believe it. Not only was it **not** off the market but was the gold standard for evaluation tools for Autism. We were stuck using whatever evaluation tools the school used. I prepared information and documentation about the pragmatics of speech which was what added to the language and socialization issues for children with Autism. Independent testing broke down all aspects of written speech. Heather did not understand sarcasm. When reading, she was literal so could not understand inferences. Edgar Allen Poe and his writing style was a foreign language to Heather which she simply would never understand. I brought a current, very thorough OT evaluation explaining the development of the Modulation Program and how the school issue needs to fulfill this. I also wanted Heather's Home-Bound Instructor to attend the meeting. The IEP process allows for anyone with knowledge of the child be allowed to attend. I'd thought if the school learned what Heather was like in the morning, they would understand. They would not allow me to bring in a video-tape or have the Home-Bound Instructor attend.

Here's Tip #13: Anyone with special knowledge about your child can, by law, be included in your IEP.

Here's Tip #14: Wisconsin State law allows you to tape-record your IEP meeting. My district would not allow this!

This Instructor explained to Heather that she was not permitted to come to the meeting even though she was personally willing to do it. The school's Director of Student Services was her boss and would not allow her to attend. She explained to Heather the repercussions of getting fired and losing her job if she didn't listen to her boss. The Home-Bound instructor **was** allowed to put in writing how many times she was scheduled to see Heather and how many times she was successful. For example, I was scheduled to meet with Heather thirty-six times and she canceled four times. Heather suggested that we write a letter to explain her morning modulation issues. I wrote the letter but my gut told me this would be a mistake. I explained that the Director of Student Services would ask why the Home-Bound Instructor didn't document that type of behavior and there would be an implication that I wasn't telling the truth. This was a no-win situation because the Home-Bound Instructor was not qualified to make those types of observations, was discouraged from doing so, wasn't allowed to attend the meetings, and thus I was on my own.

Prior to an IEP Meeting, you are asked to fill out paperwork outlining your concerns about your child. This paperwork is supposed to become part of the master paperwork. Based on their guidelines, the District then evaluates, observes, and gathers information to draw their conclusions. When I attended this particular Meeting, the District paperwork was like a checklist contradicting my concerns. The District controls the IEP and/or the 504 paperwork. Following the Meeting, they wrote the formal or legal IEP/504 and sent a copy to me. Where were my concerns? What was summarized by the school didn't resemble what I had written. Truth be told, the copies were frequently inaccurate and plagued with typographical and grammatical errors. In the school's attempt to cut and paste the IEP paperwork together, the copies for distribution to the IEP Team frequently were not identical. It made it impossible to refer to the document because not only were the pages not numbered but members had different amounts of pages.

Here is Tip #15: The Parent Concern section of the IEP paperwork is the only place the parents get to have their say. They are your words said your way. The school should not contradict your concerns or summarize them.

The paperwork was the IEP Team's process of a lesson in semantics. I learned the meaning of 'permissive language'. It implies something or redirects what is really meant. The school frequently uses words such as, "it appears", "and/or ". For example: "Your child will get supports individually **and/or** in a group environment." Well, which is it? This does not give clear understanding of the school's intentions.

Here is Tip #16: Be specific about the written words in the IEP paperwork so you have a clear understanding of what the school's commitment is for services. On the modification page it should provide the specific information of the school's commitment, location, and duration of the support. Do not accept verbiage such as; "and/or" or " individual or classroom".

We attended another long arduous meeting. As is tradition for these meetings, the school read verbatim everything out loud to the group as if they were unable to read. There was little or no time to process the mass amounts of information and we were required to respond with answers. In the section called Parent Concerns, I was required to fill this out in advance and it was supposed to be reflected in the paperwork. When the District finished rewriting, summarizing, and editing, I couldn't see my words or concerns reflected anywhere in their paperwork.

Everyone who wasn't affiliated with the District who understood Autism and the educational system and had read Heather's paperwork, all felt there was no question that Heather should qualify for IDEA, Special Education. These professionals included: WI Facets, WI Coalition of Advocacy, the two Educational Psychologists that specialized in Autism, and the Autism Specialist at CESA2.

After hours in this meeting, I got to the point where I was talking about the sensory piece again and what sensory needs Heather has and why she has them and why we're looking to do what we're doing. I also talked about Home-Bound Instruction. I addressed the letter we had written. The Director of Student Services actually told the IEP Team, just as I predicted, that they couldn't take any value into anything I was telling them. If the Home-Bound Instructor saw that behavior she would have written it. I just shook my head. There was that implication again; that I was lying.

I decided to ask the Director of Student Services a question. I asked if she had heard from Jan Serak, the Director at WI Facets. She said 'no'. I asked if Jan Serak had reached out to her in writing or via email within the last few days regarding Heather's eligibility for Special Education. Again she said 'no'. I had received a phone call the previous day from Jan Serak. She told me she had read through Heather papers and that it made no sense why she did not qualify for Special Education at least under OHI, given Heather's medical picture. She said she had had a conversation with the Director of Student Services in Heather's School District regarding this. Ms. Serak was talking about this woman across from me at the eligibility meeting. I was being lied to; I explained my conversation with Ms. Serak to the IEP Team. I was furious. This was for Heather's health and well-being. I couldn't trust this person and she's in charge! I told this to the IEP Team and I also told them that I wouldn't attend another meeting with a person whose integrity I questioned. Adding insult to injury, we are paying thousands of dollars for therapy which is being undermined. We are working with experts with Autism experience and some of the school personal barely know Heather and have limited access or training regarding her health information. I announced that the meeting was over and I walked out the door. When a meeting ends like that, it is supposed to end. I felt bad because Heather was supposed to be at school at 11:30 am and as I recall, it was about 12:20 pm. We'd been there from 8:00 am until 12:20 pm which gives you an indication of those marathon meetings.

Here is Tip #17: As stated in the IEP Process Guidelines, a parent has the right to end the meeting at any time and reconvene at a later date.

When I left, that meeting should have ended per the IEP process guidelines. Yet, I had enough time to get in my car, drive home to pick up Heather, explain what happened at the meeting, and drive back to school. As we were entering the building, we noticed that the meeting was still in progress and Heather decided that she wanted to talk to them. The School Psychologist asked us to sit down. It was a long narrow room with a rectangle table. We entered near the shorter side looking down the length of the table. Heather entered and I followed. Immediately, I saw her body language shift. She started to clench her fists, her shoulders elevated, and I could see her neck tightening. These were all signs of escalation. We'd been working a lot on body language to teach Heather clues in order to understand certain behaviors. Heather refused to sit so I stood with her. Heather said that she didn't understand that if her doctors tell her she has Autism and they give her things to do which help her, then why does the school say that she doesn't have Autism and that she doesn't need to do these things. The School Psychologist tried to explain that the educational definition of Autism differs from the medical definition. Heather asks, "If that's the case, why didn't the Director of Student Services allow my Home-Bound Instructor to come and talk about my behaviors?" The Director, hearing this, turns around so her back is to us, looks down, and says, "I never said that." We weren't privy to the conversation between the Director and the Home-Bound Instructor but we were privy to the conversation between the Home-Bound Instructor, Heather, and me. That was certainly the impression we got. Heather said, "You are a liar!" Her jaw was clenched tight. I said, "You're right. That's what I've been trying to show you, Heather; the school has a different agenda than we do. You don't have to listen to anyone in this room or this school. You have to do what the doctors taught you to do and use your sensory supports when you need them in an appropriate manner." I told her that there would be no suspension or detention. Her concern was graduating with her peers and she voiced it. I explained that we didn't need a diploma from this High School. I told her how smart she was and she knew if she could control her sensory behaviors, she could do the work. I told her that she would get a High School diploma, not a GED, but maybe a diploma from somewhere else. This entire conversation took place in front of that IEP Team. It was a bittersweet moment. We left. I vowed not to come back to **any** meetings. A very interesting thing happened. Heather started initiating her sensory supports in school in the environments she needed when she needed them regardless of whether the teachers saw the need or not. Initially, I had to field some phone calls from teachers who were talking about Heather doing supports in the classrooms. I said if they had a problem we could meet and I would provide copies of the doctor's recommendations to access the supports and if they still had a problem we could go to the Principal together and we'd find a teacher willing to allow for Heather's Sensory Supports. The calls eventually stopped.

Heather started to improve. She started being able to sustain longer in school. She reduced her absenteeism from 75 plus days a year to 23 and increased her ability to sustain from 3 ½ hours to 6 hours. She had a problem regulating herself in the mornings and still has that problem. She is not good in those hours when she first gets up whatever time it is. She was accessing the sensory supports in her classrooms on her own when she needed them regardless of what anyone said. These kind of supports helped Heather; chewing gum, chewing on a straw, molding putty in her hands before she wrote to stimulate that writing skill motor response, or smelling an essential oil to block out smells. Heather had no filter and over-registered sensory input. If she had to get up and leave the classroom for a while or not eat in the cafeteria, she did it when she needed it. She was self-accessing her sensory diet developed through the Modulation Program and the improvement was profound.

Along with the increased ability to sustain, came a longer school day so Heather was going to be put in a regular Math classroom. The first thing I decided to do was to notify the head of the Math Department and talk to him about teaching styles of the various teachers. I called the Vice-Principal because she was my 'assigned' contact at school. She told me not to contact the head of the department because that was not how they did things. I called him anyway and luckily he was a wonderful guy. [By this point, I was pretty vocal. I spoke at many Board of Education meetings along with the Staff, PTA, and the medical community. Many people reached out to help; even some teachers and support staff.] We had a nice conversation and he gave me some good advice. With his recommendation, I asked for an instructor I thought would be best suited for Heather's learning style during her senior year. When Heather was starting High School and having Math problems, my pro-active mind wanted to know about the Math Curriculum they were suggesting. I learned that it was called the Core Math Program. It was a three-year program. At the end, it was considered to have fulfilled the requirements of the completion of Algebra 1, Algebra 2, and Geometry for Post-Secondary Education for college. In reality, only University of Wisconsin schools would accept this Core Math Program. No private schools would accept this because it didn't meet Post-Secondary School guidelines for acceptance. If Heather was going to college, she would need a small private Post-Secondary Education environment so we needed to meet that Math requirement.

As a senior, Heather did not do well in the regular Math classroom. She still had non-verbal problem solving skills and couldn't write or show her work. She simply could not process the way this class was being taught. I hired a Tutor; a School District Math Teacher who wanted to stay home after her first child was born. Heather knew her and was comfortable with her. The school decided to let Heather take all of her Math work to the Tutor in order to complete her Math requirements for this class. With the Tutor, Heather could do the work but at a much slower pace with continual one-on-one support. The school decided, though, that Heather would still attend the class. She was still having struggles at school. The winter months of cold weather would shut her down. She still wasn't completely regulating her body temperature properly and this class shut her down. Heather was producing no work in the regular Math classroom but I was paying for the Tutor who actually helped her complete the Math work.

The Director of Student Services left the District and a new one had been hired. I had respect for her because she attended the conference which I co-sponsored as a parent liaison for the SPD Parent Connections Group. This is a networking group, part of the STAR Center (Sensory Training and Research), from the University of Colorado. Dr. Lucy Jane Miller at the University of Colorado is leading the cause to establish Sensory Processing Disorder as a stand-alone diagnosis. I co-sponsored this conference with the Oregon School District, the PTA at the state level, and CESA 2 to teach parents and professionals about Sensory Processing Disorders. The new Director came to the conference. She asked questions, she was engaged, and she made eye contact with me. She asked me to sit down for the required 504 Plan Accommodation Meeting and I did. This was January. I even allowed Heather to attend. It was very small with Heather, me, the Director, and the School Psychologist in attendance. It was a very civil meeting. They asked Heather how things were going. Heather was having a problem with the classroom Math. It was stress-producing and could trigger a melt-down. The only place where Math was happening was with the Tutor. Heather had an issue with the group Math Class. It simply wasn't working. At the meeting, the new Director of Student Services suggested that we remove her from the class. The school would take over the cost of the Math Tutor and hire her as Heather's Home-Bound Instructor for Math. She would complete her High School Math requirements with the Tutor, we hoped.

Here's what we learned from the attorneys that we hired. It cost $17,000.00 for them to explain to us the legal aspect of Wisconsin Special Education. As long as Heather remained under 504, the school policed itself. We had all the evaluations and documentation that showed what all the issues were surrounding the Autism diagnosis. In order for us to win our case for Special Education eligibility we would have to go to Due Process. We would lose because our medical documentation is in grade equivalent and the school's is in percentages. The State does not recognize the term grade equivalent. We'd have to appeal it, lose for the same reason to get it to the State Supreme Court. We would again lose the case for the same reason but it would then allow us to get it into federal court where we'd win. That would take roughly six to ten years and would cost approximately $25,000.00. Politicians put this process in place. We could either pay to fight the District or we could take a step back. We chose the latter.

I needed to pick my battles and luckily there were a lot of angels along the way. There were a lot of people that helped. We could see the teachers that understood and had environments in their classrooms that made it easier for Heather and other students. School personal like the Policeman in the Middle School would chat with me for a few minutes rather than yelling at me to move my car while I was picking up my child. He asked how things were going until Heather came out of the front door and got into the car.

Heather and I were walking in a grocery store one day and Heather threw her arms around somebody I didn't know. For a girl who didn't like to touch, this was pretty amazing behavior. I asked who this woman was and Heather explained that she had been an Aide in the Middle School. The Aide said that there was no denying that Heather was going through 'something' and that she needed help. This Aide tried to help her in the classroom but was told by the school that she was not there on Heather's behalf. Her efforts were appreciated though.

I don't want to blame anybody in the District or get anyone in trouble but I don't know why they acted the way they did. I don't know what motivated these people. Was the information on High-Functioning Autism too new? Was Heather too High-Functioning? Was it overzealous school administrators looking to control educational spending or was this legal discrimination? The people with children who are neuro-typically normal may sympathize but they don't truly understand. Talk to a mom with a child with Autism especially High-Functioning Autism and they understand. It's the typical story for us.

Heather's story seems like an unbelievable blur at this point but there were enough people along the way that looked out for us, gave information to us, and gave an answer at the right time when it was needed most. The whole educational fight is an ugly process. If you control the child's sensory issues, the education comes. That's the secret to educating most children with High-Functioning Autism. Put the focus where the need is the greatest. Don't underestimate how much Sensory Supports can help those adaptation skills and the ability to learn to modulate their systems. I've heard in many seminars that a child with a diagnosis of Autism could grow up to be a child with PDD (Pervasive Developmental Disorder) or Low-High Functioning Autism. A child with a diagnosis of Asperger's could as an adult look more like ADD; that's why it's called the Spectrum Disorder. If you can find the right supports at the right time, you can achieve a degree of Functioning Recovery. Awareness and education are crucial. There's potential for many other children. We need local affordable access to supports. I'd heard about people before Heather and I hope to hear about more after Heather. We still struggle with educational environments. We need freedom and access to address the various degrees and characteristics of Autism. We need current training and accessibility within educational environments. We also need educational laws and guidelines to be as current as the medical domain and for everyone to speak the same language.

Heather went on to Post-Secondary Education. She went to a technical school where she learned how to be a Nail Technician. She completed the program but does not work in the field. She is currently looking to start at a local college in the near future.

What is Functioning Recovery?

CHAPTER **5**

Functioning Recovery
What's Your Engine Speed?

> *It seems that for success in science or art, a dash of autism is essential.*
>
> *– Hans Aspergers*

Learning to Speak Heather's Language

MANY THINGS OCCURRED, many people contributed, and there were many pivotal factors in order for Heather to achieve Functioning Recovery. First of all, I want to explain what Functioning Recovery means. I will compare it to someone who has Diabetes. If a person is diabetic and they are following their diet or insulin regiment and their blood sugars are balanced, you would have no way of knowing, by looking at them, that they are diabetic. If on the other hand, they are not following their diet or insulin regiment you may observe odd behaviors such as slurred words or jerky movements. If you spent time with this person, you may observe that they eat on a regular schedule, won't eat certain foods, or they carry insulin to use. Functioning Recovery for a person with High-Functioning Autism or Asperger's Syndrome is very similar to this analogy. From the outside, they appear to be like any other neuro-typically normal person as long as they are following their sensory diet or lifestyle. If they ignore the clues from their body and don't access supports, they can display a wide range of maladaptive behaviors.

I learned that children can get a diagnosis of Low-Functioning on the Autism Spectrum and if they get the right supports prior to adulthood, their behaviors can improve so they are more like Asperger's or ADD. So, does Heather still have Autism? Yes, she does. Functioning Recovery is maintained as long as she self-accesses her supports the right way. When she does this, she functions really well. We don't see the severity of the behaviors that she had in Middle School and High School. Certain situations or events can trigger a melt-down but the few we've had over the past year are greatly reduced in duration and intensity.

What helped Heather to achieve this? Let's start with Bio-Medical Supports. We first discussed these in Chapter Three. Bio-Medical Supports systematically identified and replaced what chemicals and vitamins were missing in Heather's body. They removed the toxins and the mercury. It's not cut and dried; it's a very involved process. If there were ten children lined up with the same diagnosis on the Autism Spectrum, they could all present differently; their chemical make-up could all be different. I have an inch-thick, loose-leaf notebook from Dr. Hicks with this type of information. He explained Heather's imbalances and internal allergies. During our work with him, his practice was called Pathways Medical Advocates and now is called Elemental Living. He relocated to Delavan, WI from Grays Lake, IL which was wonderful for us because it was easier to work with him on a regular basis. In the notebook, which he gave to us, Heather's detailed chemical picture was included. The results were labeled like a bell-curve. It started with a little red mark which would transition into a little yellow area then move into the green middle areas. Then it transitioned back to yellow then red. These marks showed if something was too high or too low. Dr. Hicks explained that ideally, every mark should be in the green areas which meant that the system was working appropriately and the body had all the chemicals in the right combination to work and develop properly. Heather did not; her marks were all over the place. It was well beyond me to understand enough to explain in detail but Dr. Hicks was the expert; I followed his lead and recommendations. He was clearly knowledgeable in this area. He told me that the brain was a wonderful thing and had the ability to self-correct. By following his protocol over the course of a year, Heather's brain could jump-start itself and begin to produce some of these chemicals on her own. I asked for clarification. If Heather followed his Bio-Medical Protocols for a year, she could achieve Functioning Recovery? We were on board. Here's an example of how that impacted Heather: An important aspect for Heather was that she produced no serotonin. Serotonin is a neuro-transmitter produced in the adrenal glands. Its job is to go to the brain and keep the connections working. (This is my simplistic explanation.) According to Dr. Hicks we would replace or stimulate the body to produce more serotonin and in a year her body would produce it on its own. That would be the case for all the missing chemicals, vitamins and minerals.

We followed his protocol and recommendations. Heather was fifteen; a sophomore in High School. Her medical issues were at their worst; five-day shut-downs and the Autistic characteristics noticeably present. We started noticing improvement after a few months into the therapy. By the end of the year, there was no denying the change. Heather's skin wasn't sallow any longer; her coloring was good. Her dark circles were gone. You could see that she didn't appear as fragile. She looked healthier. She was stronger and the intensity and duration of the melt-downs lessened. There was a reduction of the phantom rashes that used to appear for no reason. Heather also seemed to be less in a fog though this issue still presented itself with increased stress or fatigue.

We also learned about Heather's lax joints and lack of muscle tone which wasn't noticeable when she was a younger child but became more noticeable as she grew into her teenage years and into adulthood. This is why she fatigued so easily and why writing was so challenging for her. Puberty is very difficult on children with Asperger's. Their chemical make-up is changing every day at a rapid pace so it's not uncommon to see big changes from the younger ages to puberty. She still has very low muscle tone and poor circulation in her legs and ankles which causes her to fatigue more quickly than most people.

Dr. Hicks and I had a long discussion on vaccines. The mercury poisoning in her body, we felt, was from vaccinations. I'm not going to go into detail about vaccines but we did see a big decline in Heather's medical make-up after her two-year-old shots and again after we started the Hepatitis Series of three shots that were required in Fifth and Sixth Grades. She didn't complete that series after I decided that this wasn't a good option for Heather. A comment about the shots: In Wisconsin where we live, there is a state law that says if your child is not current on their vaccinations, they could be excluded from school. They even advertised this law on the news but the federal government overrides this. The federal law allows you, as a parent, to make that decision for your child until the age of eighteen years old. In this case, you don't need a long drawn-out law suit; you simply sign the area on the back of the vaccination form that school sends home or send a notarized letter to the school stating that you refuse to vaccinate your child for personal beliefs. Another important thing of which to be aware is your child's age. The school, without notice to you, may opt to exclude you from meetings or input once your child reaches eighteen. A notarized letter, allowing you the decision-making rights for your child after the age of eighteen, will prevent that from happening. Schools have to honor these letters or choices.

Here is Tip #18: Prior to your child's eighteenth birthday, give the school a notarized letter allowing you to continue to have decision-making power for your child to avoid being excluded.

With recommendations from Dr. Hicks, we systematically replaced what chemicals, vitamins, and minerals which were missing from her body, chelated the mercury, and removed foods to which she was allergic. She was frequently queasy from this regiment but we persevered.

I cannot talk about Functioning Recovery without talking about Sensory Processing Disorder. I learned so much about SPD and how Heather's sensory system worked. This was a key quest to get Heather some appropriate supports in school. I did read some of the old evaluations and reports; I came across a report that Dr. Mann wrote in 1996. His was the first evaluation that was done privately and was presented to the school. We had begun our journey. I felt that I didn't know anything back then. I assumed that I would get this out-of-school evaluation, take it to the school, and they would do their best to implement it. Something in Dr.Mann's report really spoke to me. I don't know why this was overlooked by the school but here's an excerpt from the report: "One thing to be kept in mind is Heather's stress producing surgical history. Emerging clinical research data suggests that stress-inducing life events in childhood have a developmental impact on neuro-transmitter receptors in the brain. This means that sensory input may need to be stronger in one or more of the sensory input areas. Heather can be taught to be quickly aware of stress reactions in her body and the subsequent application of stress management exercises which will moderate the autonomic arousal which will most likely affect the processing of new information in challenging situations."

Every year that a child who goes without appropriate Sensory Supports in their environment, it takes twice as long to reeducate them. So, when I came across that report and read that one particular recommendation, I drew the conclusion that the information about Asperger's and Sensory Processing Disorders was fairly new and that's why the School Psychologist ignored it in 1996. Why was this still being ignored when Heather was in High School? I initially didn't understand Dr.Mann's report but I understand it now. Its implication makes me wonder how differently Heather's story would be if she received Sensory Supports in school back in 1996.

While reflecting back, had we provided some Sensory Supports when she needed them at a younger age, perhaps her scenario would not have turned out to be so life-threatening. I don't dwell on that. I think everyone is on their journey for a reason and we are very grateful that we came out of the fog onto the other side.

I saw how helpful the Sensory Supports were. At home, I created Heather's Sensory Environment. We painted her room per her guidelines. She had blue walls with fluffy clouds, butterflies and flowers, the ceiling was one massive sun, and the lower part of her room was a darker blue with glow-in-the-dark suns and moons and stars. We filled our house with Sensory Supports; fiddle toys, bouncy balls, trampolines, and access to swings. We did the brushing program and we purchased, from our OT, an auditory listening program called <u>The Listening Program</u>. We revisited that program a few times during the "lost years". It helped to improve her auditory processing issues. Ms. Kratz taught us that she was still young and some of the sensory differences could actually be rehabilitated. The degree of rehabilitation is different for every person. A sensory diet or lifestyle teaches the child and the parent which Sensory Supports are helpful, which are not, and when to access them. Initially, Heather relied on the adults around her to cue her to her need to access a support.

Here's Tip #19: A child with Autism is impacted medically if they are not receiving regular one-on-one OT support in school to build a sensory diet and it could affect their ability to achieve Functioning Recovery.

Ms. Kratz taught my husband and me how to be detectives and we were good students. She called it Behavior-Neurology. We learned to understand what Heather's behaviors were telling us. They were clues to her functioning. We learned that Heather was a literal learner so we became more literal in our approach. To avoid triggering a melt-down, we learned we would tell Heather, for example, not the time of the doctor's appointment but what time we had to leave the house. If we said that we had a 9:00 am appointment, Heather's processing mind registered that time. A melt-down would ensue if at 8:30 am we were telling her we had to leave.

Here is Tip #20: Children with Autism don't understand lapsed time. A visual timer can be very helpful; they are designed so the child can see that time is elapsing.

This is why parents have to learn how their child functions. My friend Pattie and her two boys came to visit and swim one day. Her youngest, Nathan, is on the Spectrum. Nathan started saying, "Curious George crosses his legs." I was baffled to understand what he meant but his mom knew. He had to use the bathroom. Like this mom, I learned to understand Heather's language. I learned how to communicate looking at behavior clues as guidelines.

We applied these techniques to help Heather educationally. When we saw a deficit area, we addressed that specifically. For example, we learned through evaluations that Heather did not understand sarcasm and metaphors. We found a way to teach that. We provided, as recommended, a structured, organized, and predictable environment at home. The area in which we had no control, was arranging these supports at school. Some children are home-schooled. They simply can't adapt. Again, it was not the right option for us.

We had a wonderful medical team. My husband and I worked with two pediatricians, a local doctor, and an Autism Specialist, an OT, a SLP for pragmatics of speech, and an endocrinologist. We worked together to figure out what was best and what areas needed to be addressed. Socialization was one of those areas. *(Refer to Appendix E for Social Networking Resources)* We'd also heard, along the way, that socialization was like a muscle, if you didn't use it you would lose it or not develop the skills. Where does a child socialize but in school? We continually looked for opportunities for Heather to socialize. We found success even in failed opportunities because we learned more about what Heather could or could not tolerate. Role playing games is supposed to be very beneficial and we were doing those for years before her diagnosis. Reality TV, for us, was the best teaching tool for appropriate and inappropriate behaviors.

Here is Tip #21: Now, there are programs like <u>Floortime</u> and <u>RDI</u> (Relationship Development Intervention) that help and teach social skills.

The Mental Health Provider was doing a great job. Heather's self-esteem improved, things became a lot easier at home, and the symptoms of OCD and ODD lessened. This Provider also helped us learn about some of Heather's in-the-heat-of-the-moment situations which she was unable to articulate to us. Having a good working rapport with your medical team is invaluable. It only works if you all work together.

Heather was increasing her body awareness. In fact, it was during this time that she was able to explain what was going on in her head while exhibiting her tic. She explained she had to trace a random number or letter in her head perfectly or she had to repeat the process until it was flawless. Heather really related to a movie that the two of us were watching one day. It was entitled, <u>Mozart and the Whale</u>. It's a story with actor, Josh Hartnett. He leads a group of people whom we presume have Asperger's and sensory issues at various functioning levels. We watched how Josh Hartnett's character would see a number and all of a sudden, it would stop him. He would get stuck in his head and would have to multiply numbers over and over. Heather remarked how that was a lot like how it was for her. She was right; it was like a short in a circuit. She looked like she got stuck in her tic and then she would trace those numbers and letters in her head. That is what Heather was like. This really bright girl has glitches in her thinking that do not correlate to the intelligence she possesses. We encouraged her to listen to her body and to do some relaxation and calming techniques. Though tactile defensive for years, she now responds well to massage and reflexology to calm her.

Heather started to open up about what it felt like for her. She said school for her was like acting and role playing. Heather played the character of a 'regular person'. Heather said it took all of her energy just to act like she was normal. This showed us how much energy and stress was put on her to maintain that persona.

Ms. Kratz explored ways to change Heather's sensory state. We needed information from the school that we didn't have because we weren't there. At this point, this was Heather's typical week: She went to school 3 ½ hours a day. She was able to function at a maximum of 20-25 hours a week. If she was already going to school 17 ½ hours, how did she sustain beyond that for therapy, socialization, homework, or Synagogue? We learned to work within the hours that Heather could sustain. A normal student goes to school for 35 hours a week. They might spend another 2-3 hours after school with sports or clubs and maybe another 10 hours a week at a job. Look at the difference; Heather could only sustain less than half that amount of time.

We picked our battles at home. If Heather wanted to wear dance clothes because Spandex gave her that deep pressure sensory support, we were okay with that. She wore the same kind of clothes all the time. Sometimes we would buy three or four pairs of the same thing because it was about the feel not so much as the look. We were grateful when manufacturers started adding Spandex to denim and cotton clothing. Some children with Asperger's are very overt. If you touch them, they scream. Heather wasn't like that even though she had some touch or tactile defensiveness. Our observations showed that it was subtle but a build-up would increase over time. Ten kids bumping into her was not a problem but continual bumping through the course of the day would shut her down. Many factors influenced this: amounts of schoolwork, scheduled tests, weather shifts, or how crowded the environment. For example: When Heather was in Elementary School, it didn't really appear to be a problem but that environment had approximately 400 students in fairly nurturing self-contained classrooms, minimal movement in crowded hallways, and different teachers for Gym, Art, and Music. Things are usually calm and friendly. When they enter Middle School, the student population is approximately 600 students and classes are changed for each subject. Heather was assigned a "house" where they were contained in a section of a hallway. Every student in her "house" had the same core teachers. By the time the students go to High School, they're with 2,000 students. They have 7 minutes in a crowded hallway to get from one end of the school to the other. How many students are bumping into each other over the course of a single day? You can't walk down the hall without being bumped. The child with SPD in the area of tactile defensiveness feels an assault every time they are bumped.

Here is Tip #22: Allowing your child with Tactile Defensiveness to leave class five minutes before it ends, should allow your child to get through the school hallways before the entire student body is released.

At home where we controlled the environment, we saw huge improvements but we had no control over the school environment.

We were looking to them for insights into her day. Some things we could easily solve. We looked at finger foods. When Heather was younger, she ate with her fingers quite often. She would rather do that than use a fork. At home, we let it slide but it wasn't acceptable at school or in public. The older she got the more difficult it was to send finger foods to school. The way in which Heather ate was not acceptable. No parent wants their child to be bullied or picked-on so we set parameters about the types of food which could be eaten. Her choices had to fit certain healthy guidelines. The food had to be all natural and couldn't be boxed or pre-packaged. We learned to make soup for Heather; we would use chicken broth, a meat broth, and a pasta product mixed with some chicken or vegetables. She loved Hot and Sour soup. She ate it four to five times a week. Soup and sunflower seeds were her diet. We kept the bucket of seeds, full at all times, so she could help herself at any hour of the day. This is typical of a child with Asperger's; they like to eat the same foods prepared the same way over and over again. It was healthy. It had tofu and vegetables in it and no msg. (a sodium based preservative). If she wanted to eat that type of food every day of the week, it didn't matter to us. It calmed Heather to follow this regiment.

Here is Tip #23: Children with Autism like structure, routine, and to follow rituals.

Quite often Heather had her fingers in her mouth when she was younger. This is not appropriate as the child gets older. She liked to push on the roof of her mouth. It was calming for her. I mentioned earlier, this helped to release the exact part of her cranial base where the gland was that produced those life-threatening levels of stress hormones. I don't know if it was a connection or not but if it relieved and calmed her down, it became an appropriate thing to do at home.

We looked at what would be appropriate things to do in school. She could chew on a straw, she could drink water, and she could chew gum. The school had a 'no gum policy' so we had to work through that. They wanted her to suck on candy all the time. We didn't want to give candy to our child with ADHD. Pumping her full of sugar was not an option. We had to find a solution where we could both agree; clearly this sensory diet was working and we continued to clash with the school in regards to what was happening at school. Even with the disagreements with the District Administration, teachers were invaluable to us. Even those that were clearly not trained started pointing things out to me that they saw. I am forever grateful to them for all of the little clues that they gave to us.

When I watched the auto-biographical movie <u>Temple Grandin</u>, she had just started to become well-known for her Asperger's which was unique in itself. Most people with Asperger's are boys with a ratio of four out of five but Temple is a college professor in Animal Behavior Science and wrote a book called <u>Thinking in Pictures.</u> When I looked at her, I saw how stiff and robotic she was. Her speech was called pedantic or same monotone. Heather didn't present quite like that because we had noticed and worked on some of those traits early on. When Heather didn't make eye contact, we taught her how to do that. Parts of my family are entertainers. We are animated, we talk with a lot of inflection in our voices, and we noticed Heather responded well to role-playing. So we used that to teach her inflection. Her voice didn't have that robotic monotone, pedantic sound. Her movements were still stiff though. A wonderful drama coach in Ninth Grade noticed this and thought that he could really help with that issue. Drama classes became a huge help for Heather. In fact, the Drama Teacher came to me and asked if I would let Heather audition for the school play. I knew that any unnecessary input would make things that much worse but they were doing the play <u>The Miracle Worker</u> about Helen Keller. Heather was very excited. We hadn't seen her happy or excited about anything in a long while. Parents want their children to have positive experiences. I said that we could try. We'd see how it goes. Imagine my surprise, though, when she auditioned and got the lead as Helen

Keller. The coach thought that Heather's disability might actually be an asset for her with her acting. She could use some of those feelings to get out some frustrations. Administration was concerned about the impact of learning lines but Heather only had one line. I have to say that it was amazing to see. The more Heather was involved in Theater, the less stiff she became in her movements. If you met her now, you'd be hard-pressed to recognize any of that.

Ms. Kratz figured out how Heather's Sensory System worked. The next step was to try to develop a modulation program. The Program she wanted to use was called How Does Your Engine Run? You can Google this; it's pretty well-known. It's a visual teaching tool. Here's my description: There are three train cars lined up; the engine in front, a box car in the middle, and a caboose at the end. A picture of your child is placed in the middle box car so he/she realizes that they are in the middle of the train. If his/her system is going too fast, the question is asked, "What's your engine speed?" A child would be taught to visually identify if he/she was the engine who was pulling everyone, the caboose that was being dragged along, or the middle box car which was just right. That's how I understood the program to work. As a High School student, Heather thought this Program was too juvenile. Ms. Kratz allowed her pick what she would use to identify her sensory state. She used smiley faces. The face in the middle was happy. The face on the right was bad, depressed, not moving, and wore a frown. The face on the left was agitated with a squiggly-lined mouth. We learned to say over and over, "Where's your system at?" This is a multi-step program. First the child learns to identify their sensory state; then they encourage the use of the Sensory Supports that can increase or decrease that sensory state. The goal, of course, is to reduce shut-down or overt behaviors and to teach the child to self-access the supports without adult prompting.

It was important to learn the signs of escalation or melt-down and to let the parents and the teachers, who work with the child, become aware of them. The child needs to be educated in their sensory state and to be taught how to self-access supports or self-stimulation to counterbalance the current sensory state. We created a modulation program in our home environment. Yes, there were times I wanted to punish Heather for not doing something but I had to recognize when her sensory state was not open for more input. I had to learn to wait until she was in a better state. Then I was able to go back and discuss what Heather did wrong and give consequences for bad behavior. We applied this technique when working with social clues. When she attended a social event, we knew that she would isolate herself from others. We knew the ramifications of this would affect us at home. Her Autistic characteristics escalated and she became more rigid, more inflexible, and less cooperative. This is the girl who spent hours in a closet when she was younger. We wanted to keep her engaged, focused, continuing to try, and out of that closet. We all attended a family wedding together. The fact that she attended was an improvement but for three days after the event, Heather could not be hugged or touched. We had to respect that. We just recently attended a wedding. On the way there, I could hear the edge in her voice. She started to negotiate when we would leave the event. She was bargaining for an hour. In the past, had I not agreed with her, she would have been so anxious about socialization, she would fly into a rage. This time, I was able to say to her, "I can't give you a time. I know and respect that you have socialization issues." She respected what I had said. She didn't fly into a rage, we stayed 3 ½ hours, and she didn't isolate herself for days afterwards. This is Functioning Recovery for Heather.

I continue to hear stories of incidents that happened years ago. I just heard a story from Heather the other day about why she hated sleepovers. When she was fourteen years old, I encouraged her to attend a sleepover. That's what girls do. I got a call by 8:00 am; she wanted to come home. She was shut down. We didn't see her for a couple of days after that. I just found out that the girl who had the sleepover was angry that Heather wanted to go to sleep. The little hostess threatened to pick on Heather while she was sleeping. Imagine how that heightened her sensory system. There are two aspects to the central nervous system. There's the Parasympathetic Nervous System. This system is responsible to help the body rest and relax. It calms you down. The Sympathetic Nervous System is your fight-or-flight response. Ms. Kratz taught us that these children with sensory issues are in a heightened state of fight-or-flight. Heather needed to not feel that response. She never did choose "flight" but she articulated that desire in High School.

In Tenth Grade, the School decided to have their OT speak to Heather about her sensory issues. The OT and the Guidance Counselor took her to a small office wide enough for a desk and a few chairs. I don't know what the conversation was because I wasn't there. Afterwards in counseling, I learned that Heather wanted to jump out of the window. She said that the OT was contradicting what Ms. Kratz had said. She wanted to get away. Clearly, I needed to be more involved in these kinds of school interactions. Perhaps their lack of training instigated this response from Heather. She had never articulated this "flight" response while working with the trained medical professionals. I couldn't trust that the school personal, even Heather's Support Team, were trained or experienced enough to communicate in an appropriate manner with a child with Autism.

We knew a young child with Asperger's (on the Spectrum) who needed a twelve foot girth between him and someone else when he was escalating into a melt-down. He got so overwhelmed in school, he took off. He would run two miles to his mom's shop and hide in the back before the Police car got there. Luckily, this mother knew enough to give her child the space he needed to calm down and work on defusing that scenario. The Police began to understand and appreciate what the mom was saying. Heather had many of those fight-or-flight feelings. If a person didn't understand the disability, didn't speak to her appropriately, or didn't recognize certain signs, anyone could escalate her into a frightened state. I emphasize the word **frightened** because of those life-threatening stress hormones. This same bright, intelligent, articulate child could end up on the floor in a fetal position not able to speak in sequential order. We needed to make sure that she didn't escalate to that state. So, we followed the advice of Ms. Kratz.

As the school was denying supports, they were giving us clues they didn't even realize they were giving. Much of the IEP paperwork was the school trying to prove that my concerns were unfounded. I talked about the socialization piece and how from eleven to eighteen years old, she didn't really have friends. Even today, she really has very few friends and is quite often alone. I looked outside of the school since they would not agree to Peer Supports. This was one of the recommendations from the UW system; they talked about using Peer Supports to teach appropriate social skills for a teenager. Heather didn't do well with her peers and most of her peers didn't do well with her. I explored local colleges and past teachers from her Dance Class. We met a girl through the dance program and she helped us a lot. She did typical teenage things with Heather. The thing about teaching social behavior is you want to teach the difference between inappropriate behaviors as well as appropriate behaviors. Again, I want to thank reality television. I feel Heather did most of her improvement in social skills after High School because of watching these types of shows. We analyzed the social situations in these reality shows. We talked about what was appropriate and what was inappropriate. People who have watched reality television know that there are much more inappropriate behaviors than appropriate behaviors which gave us fuel for discussions. Those shows became a good asset for us along with the Peer Supports.

Here's an example of how the school gave us clues: For the second IEP Evaluation Process, the school wanted to do observational work. I remember the observer saying, "Heather doesn't have a problem with socialization." She went on to tell us that she had observed Heather in the hall between classes. The observer was concerned that Heather would be late for class because she said 'hello' to many students. Approximately fifteen children greeted her. A child with Autism and an OCD component will respond to everyone who stops her, to say 'hello' and 'how are you?' I took this information and the current evaluations, which the school had done, to my Autism experts. They said that this wasn't a sign of socialization; it was a clear sign of Heather's Autism. If ten children stopped to say 'hello' to Heather in the hallway, Heather would respond to those ten children. If fifteen children said 'hello', Heather would stop and respond to those fifteen children. That's the type of thing that would side-track Heather. Twenty or thirty people could stop and say 'hello' and Heather would respond to them. She didn't have it in her to say, "gotta run" or "can't talk". She complained that it was the other students' fault. We teach that it's appropriate to return a 'hello' when somebody says' hello' to you. Heather exhibited those skills and manners. Here is an example of the school not understanding the information we needed to help Heather: There were teachers telling me that they had actually incorporated little Sensory Supports for other kids and found success for those students as well. One teacher told me that she had a student that was very difficult and wasn't successful in an auditorium environment. He was always very fidgety, out of control, and disruptive. She had to sit by him and frequently he was removed from the Auditorium. She handed him one of the fiddle toys to keep his hands moving and he was able to make it through the auditorium event.

Heather did well in the classroom environments where teachers understood. We hired the teachers that seemed to have a really good rapport with Heather and she responded well, too. I noticed her educational skills were regressing from one grade to the next. We hired School District teachers in the summer to keep Heather on track. We eventually hired a High School Math Teacher on maternity leave to get her through Math requirements. They were very helpful and we tried to implement as much support into her life as possible.

We gave Heather visual organizers so she could keep her paperwork together and in-check. We tried to find ways to allow her to have a quiet area in school and avoid areas that shut her down, like the cafeteria. These were some of the things that I learned in the trainings that I had attended. I learned that we needed to build a Support Team around a child with Autism so they felt like they had someone safe to go to. It was important to choose school personal that were trained in Autism. If they were trained in the characteristics of Heather's disability, they could actively seek to help Heather deescalate.

Heather took Driver Education. We hired the D. E. Teacher to provide private lessons for four years. We worked diligently with Heather to help her achieve that goal. It wasn't that she wasn't smart enough to drive but with her sensory system, we had learned that the area which affected Heather was the Vestibular System or her sense of balance. So, picture yourself sitting behind the wheel of a car. As you lift your right foot, your hands are turning the wheel and your body shifts. We take it for granted. Our body automatically balances out when we turn that wheel. For Heather, that was awkward. She could not do that; her Vestibular System did not respond the right way. We used the same Sensory Supports. We suggested weighted items to give Heather that sense of proprioception or deep pressure so she felt more balanced. Heather opted for loud music on the radio with the bass boosted on high. The Driver Education Teacher was very accommodating. In fact, he was also the Gym Teacher from the Middle School which was so helpful. I was grateful for his help. One day, it just came to Heather. If she leaned back in the seat, she felt more grounded. She understood that and now could turn the wheel of a car and not slide around on the seat. These were important things for Heather to learn about her body awareness and what she needed. We didn't argue with her. We looked for appropriate ways for her to get the sensory input she needed to keep her system balanced. When she first got her license, we feared that she would be out somewhere and her system would shut down. How would she drive? When Heather said, "It's not a good day for me to drive", we respected that even when she looked so strong and healthy. We couldn't tell by looking at her that there was a problem but she was experiencing it.

Here is Tip #24: Front-loading is an important support to reduce anxiety from a change in routine. It's a heads-up to the child with Autism that their regular routine is changing. The key is to allow adequate front-loading time; each child may require a different amount of time to process the change. For example, letting the child know right before the change may not allow their brains enough time to process.

Front-loading is important because people with Asperger's like structure, routine, and they do not like change. If there's going to be a change in the schedule, giving the child a 'heads-up' can avoid escalating or triggering a melt-down or outburst. At home, this was easy to implement but not at school. For example, the High School decided to allow the local Police to do a bomb-scare lock-down drill. We got a letter that basically said that sometime in the following week, there would be a simulation of a lock-down at the school. Children will not be allowed to leave. Parents will not be able to get in. The phones will not be answered. The drill was to last a couple of hours. It isn't that I didn't appreciate the need to practice such a drill; I surmised it would be a sudden change in routine and would feel chaotic and disorientating to Heather. This was happening at the same time when the doctors had told us that Heather produced life-threatening levels of stress hormones to which she had no control. This event could be a sudden stress trigger. Melt-downs were lasting for days. I notified my contact for Heather at the school which was the Vice-Principal. I voiced my concerns. I did not want Heather to miss school so if she could give us a 'heads-up' on which day the drill would happen, I wouldn't send Heather to school that day. The Vice-Principal couldn't tell me. She told me that if she did, she could lose her job and it was supposed to be as 'real life' as possible. The school had been given strict instructions on how this was to be handled and a list of reasons why she couldn't tell me. I understood and requested Heather's school work for the following week. Under these circumstances, I would not be sending Heather to school. The school was not happy. On Monday, I didn't send Heather to school. I started to get phone calls. Heather had one really good friend who was very accepting of her condition; her brother also had Asperger's. She called and said, "I'm just warning you. The lock-down is happening today." I also got calls from teachers who said, "It's happening today… in a couple of hours". Those were our teacher-angels who provided and helped Heather along the way. They make me smile even today.

About forty-five minutes before the event was supposed to occur, the Vice-Principal called and said," Now, would be a good day to pick up Heather because we're going to do the lock-down." She was shocked to hear that I had already heard and wanted to know from whom. I wouldn't reveal the names of those special teachers. Heather was home working on her school assignments and we by-passed a potential meltdown trigger. Heather was able to attend school the following day.

In the past, Heather needed a couple of days advance notice of changes in her routine and schedule. Now, just a few hours are needed and on a really good day, very little notice is required.

On the road to Functioning Recovery, she was over-registering sensory input in her body. It was like constant over-stimulation with no filter. The more Heather understood, the easier it became to work with her. Now, we live, breath, and eat Sensory Processing. We now look at new environments to see if it is something Heather feels she can handle. I would sometimes visit ahead of time so I could front-load the information; where it is, what it looks like, certain kind of smells, if it's open, if it has windows, etc. so she could have some understanding of the environment. I remember looking at the local YMCA. We were looking for an indoor heated pool to see if this would help Heather to better regulate her temperature in the winter. The YMCA is located in an old building and the staircase to get to the pool was not enclosed. It was easy to see through the steps and the backs were open. Heather has no spatial awareness along with poor eyesight. She wouldn't be able to walk down those stairs without help. I'd have to be right in front of her with her hand on my shoulder taking one step at a time. To my knowledge, she has never walked down open stairs alone and avoids environments that have them. The more we keep her calm, the more the Autistic-like characteristics became manageable; they have subsided and actually almost disappeared. Also, speaking in sequential order, for example, is a characteristic I have not seen in years. Heather may have a melt-down but she can now get her words and sentences out in the correct order.

Tip #25: Many children with Autism have ocular motor issues. The eyes do not work together. It can affect their ability to read and move about their environment. Not all eye doctors are trained to evaluate for ocular motor skills.

Heather is now twenty-five years old. She has lived, for the most part, independently for the past three years. In the summer of 2012, she decided to look at options for purchasing her own home.

We took all the little clues that we had gathered and all the information that we pulled together from everywhere we could and taught Heather how to modulate her system. Our teaching network included her OT, her father, me, the social worker, the endocrinologist, the educational psychologists, the pediatricians, Wi Facets, my two best friends, and every parent before me who provided clues. She finally accessed those supports in the environments that she needed them. She especially learned to access them at school. I, honestly, can't tell you specifically what some of them were for school. Heather worked with Ms. Kratz in regards to those. She was given choices about which ones she could access. I know that she liked to chew on the plastic ring of a water bottle when she was doing Math. I knew that she liked to use therapeutic putty prior to writing. The school finally relented. Heather drank and chewed gum. Whatever she needed to do in her environment was done; even getting up to leave if she was over-stimulated. She talked about how some days, at school, she was afraid of being called on because she wasn't put together enough to formulate an answer. Instead of a complete shut-down, here was a middle step. Heather found success with the teachers that learned to respect this.

At the height of getting supports, Heather was seeing two pediatricians (a local one and an Autism Specialist), a social worker, a child psychologist, a psychiatrist, and an OT. The Bio-Medical Supports were happening regularly. She was having CranioSacral Therapy appointments. She was seeing an endocrinologist, a neurologist, an independent SLP, and had a tutor for school.

We persevered with the school. We fought for many things or found ways to get around it to get what we needed. Ultimately, we even decided it was more important for Heather to learn to modulate at school than to worry about how the school felt about the sensory supports. We instructed her to try to let the teacher know but if she felt like she was going to crash into a melt-down, she was to go directly to the Attendance Office and call me to be picked up. I learned to read the anxiety in her voice. Luckily, events happened at school and Heather took ownership of her Modulation Program.

As Heather improved, Supports and Therapies lessened. We got to the point through Functioning Recovery that she was only seeing her OT and Social Worker, having CranioSacral Therapy regularly, and doing Bio-Medical Supports.

At least to me, Functioning Recovery wasn't about just getting Heather through puberty and High School. There was a European study done years ago when I initially started my journey. I read that approximately 90+% graduated from High School; 70% of those were able to make it through college but that less than 40% could live independently. The sad thing for me to read was by their late 20's, 95% of them claimed that they had no friends.

I still felt we had a ways to go before Functioning Recovery. I wanted Heather to live independently, have a job, go to college, and to be able to socialize. That is her level of Functioning Recovery. Some children with Autism do better with home-schooling and aren't able to live independently. We were exploring avenues for Heather to have some level of employment that would work around her sensory needs so we worked on some independent living skills. She rented her first apartment which was on the second story of an old house. We learned a lot from this first experience. Some may say that it was a failed attempt but we learned more information about Heather. That pesky Vestibular System couldn't function in that old building. Heather's system wouldn't calm down because she could feel the building moving. Her second apartment was in the basement floor of a two-family house. She now knows to look for a living environment that suits her sensory needs.

Heather has had various jobs. Because the role-playing skill was such a strong adaptive skill for her, her customer service skills are excellent. The role of a customer service provider is to be polite, to service your call, and to sell the product. She worked at Pizza Hut for years and did a great job. Then, she worked at Blockbuster for years and again did an excellent job. Each of these new work environments brought a different array of sensory components that we had to address. Heather was kept 'on the phones' at Pizza Hut to take orders because they were getting all kinds of calls about her excellent customer service skills on the phone. That loud, high-energy, fast-paced environment impacted her ability to settle down after work. She'd call me at the end of her shift and would scream; it sounded like a freight train was attacking me. In every single environment, she had to learn how to modulate and bring herself down.

Heather is a movie enthusiast so Blockbuster was a great job for her. She can tell you details about movies and critique them. Her customer service skills were excellent because of this. She had that job for a number of years. In fact, when one of the stores closed, leaving only one other store open in town, Heather was one of the few employees that were transferred to the other store because of her customer service skills. That OCD piece about movies really helped her in that job. To this day, she's a movie nut. Here's a piece of Asperger's though: Blockbuster closed and though there's another movie rental store in town she wouldn't apply. She was too afraid they wouldn't do things the way Blockbuster did them. Heather now has a job as a server in a casual dining restaurant. Again, she uses her great customer service skills. The role-playing game of 'the servers' role she plays well and they are reflected in her tips. It's a wonderful thing.

As always she has to learn how to modulate. After her first night of being 'on the floor', she was exhausted. Waitresses run and run and run and then they give you a break. They're exhausted. Here's a person with Asperger's who can't modulate her system. I got a call from her and I could tell that she was in the bathroom because of the echo. I could tell that she was escalating into a melt-down by the tone in her voice. A certain 'tone' would mean that she was on the floor and collapsing. It wasn't that serious but she was certainly escalating. The first thing I said to her, "Wait. I am not your intervention. I'm not there. What can you do?" I started listing suggestions. She could push on her thighs or squeeze her arms together and give herself that deep pressure she needs to calm herself. She could push on the walls. She learned a technique during CranioSacral Therapy called 'still-pointing'. It's the same idea as rebooting a computer. If you shut your computer off for a few minutes and then turn it back on, it reconfigures. 'Still-pointing' your cranial-sacral system does the same thing. It reboots; it calms the nervous system hence calms the body. She could try that. I don't know what support she accessed but she finished out her shift and came home. We have to learn to respect when she says that she can't do this or can't do that. She needs to schedule daily down-time to keep her mind and body working. Heather won't ever be able to work full time. Her sensory system did not rehabilitate to that level. She can work about twenty-five hours a week and can sustain about fifty hours total for work, play, and life-sustaining functions i.e. shopping, doctors, etc. After she graduated from High School, she applied for disability benefits. We hand-delivered the same evaluations we had given to the school and applied for benefits. I was surprised that in a county where 75% of claims are denied, ours was approved.

Currently, Heather is off all pharmaceutical drugs for anxiety, depression, ADD, OCD, ODD and the Autism. She doesn't see an OT on a regular basis anymore though I do speak with Ms. Kratz and did for a number of years just to help problem solve. Heather hasn't seen an OT in a few years. She doesn't see a neurologist or an endocrinologist. She occasionally sees a psychologist to work through a specific problem or event such as getting up the nerve to move out on her own.

As I mentioned earlier, Heather is now twenty-five years old and has lived independently for the past three years. She just recently purchased her own home not too far from our home. Having found some grant funding for a down payment, she closed on her own home in December of 2012. She maintains her own finances and holds down her job working twenty-five hours a week. She works on socialization regularly and still strives to have a close circle of friends. For a person with Asperger's Syndrome, High-Functioning Autism, this is Functioning Recovery!

CHAPTER **6**

It Takes a Village to Raise a Child
A Beautiful Pink Bundle

> *A treatment method or educational method that will work for one child may not work for another child. The one common denominator for all of the young children is that early intervention does work and it seems to improve the diagnosis.*
>
> – *Temple Grandin*

Becoming Parents

IF AT TIMES I spoke negatively about teachers, I did not write this book to bash them. I have great respect for teachers and what they do on a day-to-day basis without the support they need in the classroom. It's the educational system that's broken. I, merely, told our story. This is our journey and how we attempted to navigate the system. I didn't mention names of those who weren't helpful, weren't trained, or did things because of lack of training. There is a lot of controversy surrounding Autism these days. I have heard many stories from parents, who have children on the Autism Spectrum, about their educational experiences. Our story is not unique except that we had a positive outcome. Many families do not. This is the typical journey and struggles for parents trying to raise a child on the Autism Spectrum especially in small-town America.

> If they can't learn the way we teach, we teach
> the way they learn.
>
> – O. Ivar Lovaas

I will be forever grateful for the teachers who came forward to help even though they were told otherwise or didn't have appropriate training. Heather's Seventh Grade year was successful because of two stand-out teachers. A Social Studies/Advisory Teacher taught me to encourage Heather to write (her weak area) about things which interested her and how to break down the process into smaller steps. This teacher, who was raising his own child with disabilities, understood. I would come to learn that this was the exact educational approach to motivate a child with Autism; to be able to write and keep them engaged. The School Administration used this report that Heather wrote as an example of her ability and why she didn't need supports at school. I learned that she had this ability only under the right conditions. A Language Arts Teacher (whose husband was a Psychologist and worked with children with Autism) created a safe, structured, calm, and nurturing environment that helped Heather function well in her class. Heather would refer to this classroom environment and it became the model we looked for in later grades.

We also received backing from the Gym/Driver Education Teacher who consoled Heather and notified me later that her Science Teacher called her stupid in front of the entire class. Of course I was angry with the Science Teacher. How would that teacher know that Heather didn't understand sarcasm? He was young and had little experience. By this point, the administrators were not allowing open lines of communication between the teachers and me. So, to give him the benefit of the doubt, I will think he was being sarcastic. Heather ran out of his classroom in hysterics. I only knew something was amiss because of her melt-down behavior after school. She couldn't articulate it. Thank goodness for that Gym Teacher. I learned to ask for a daily checklist of what school was like for Heather. Some schools use a notebook that is passed back and forth between school and parents; my school finally agreed to a checklist. It never did provide the information I needed so I was continually calling and talking to teachers. The ones who communicated the most with me and were listening to what I was saying about Heather found the most success.

In High School, I had teachers who told me they saw how giving Heather a fiddle toy option calmed her down. They started handing a fiddle toy to other students that exhibited similar nervousness which also calmed them down. I can't forget those High School teachers who kept me in the loop about events at school that might have impacted her. It allowed us to make a knowledgeable choice to send Heather to school. Could she handle it? Could she handle it with some supports? Sometimes we chose to not send her at all. We didn't get this type of compassion from the administrators and were frequently told not to talk directly with the teachers. Too many students and so few support staff could be the issue. In a school district of approximately 10,000 students at the time, there were three OT's to service the entire District. My daughter's school did not have a School Nurse on site; nor was there an OT, PT, or SLP. These medically licensed school employees worked with students at multiple schools. Heather's Middle School Nurse worked at many Elementary Schools as well as in a County Nurse position. There was only one School Psychologist for 2,000 students. These are political educational issues which impact our children. Here's an example of the internal communication glitches. Remember the story of how Heather completed her Math requirements in High School? My daughter with Functioning Recovery just told me this information while writing this chapter. Heather was pulled out of her Earth Science Final to be told that she was missing so many Math assignments that she'd have to get an 85% or better on the final or she would fail the class and not graduate. They scheduled the Math Final for the following day. She can't remember who told her this because the information "freaked her out". Later we discovered it was from the Vice-Principal and the classroom Math Instructor. Heather had been dismissed from this Math class in January in favor of a district-paid Home-Bound Instructor. Did they not read Heather's 504 Plan? Did they know that the new Guidance Counselor and the Home-Bound Instructor 1) had agreed to accept and grade her in Math based on what was accomplished? Heather was three chapters behind the classroom curriculum but had fulfilled the minimum requirements for completion of the class. 2) had told Heather she had already earned an 'A' for the Math Class with her Home-Bound Teacher but just needed to take the final? 3) had already given Heather her final schedule two weeks prior that did not include her Math Final being scheduled for the following day in a classroom environment that would shut her down? The Vice-Principal and the classroom teacher knew none of this. I called the classroom teacher but she couldn't help. She said that she still had Heather on her roster and she was requiring Heather to complete the work regardless of her 504 Plan. I called the Vice-Principal but while waiting on a response, I called the Director of Student Services downtown. Heather was pulled out of a final? Does anyone else see a problem with this? I did! I heard from the Director of Student Services at least twenty-four hours sooner than I heard from the Vice-Principal. This information was presented in such an inappropriate manner that it triggered the start of a melt-down. Heather held it together for the Earth Science Final but told me that she wasn't sure as to how she did it. I was scheduled to pick her up after this final so I thought she was in her quiet sensory state from the exam. I didn't know she knew about the Math issue yet. I told her about the phone call from the Vice-Principal and explained that I was waiting to hear from the Director of Student Services. I made light of possible missing assignments. I was trying to front-load her and lighten the melt-down but when she got home, she imploded. I saw her go into her room; the isolation was very much a part of her melt-downs.

I watched as she closed herself off in her sensory-safe room. This was a typical High-Functioning Autism response. A neuro-typical student would have told their parent when they got into the car. Heather was fighting to control her Autism and anxiety in order to process what this might mean for her. Did I not spend the last four years talking to this school about anxiety issues and basic support steps for a student with Autism? The school decided to give Heather an F on five Math assignments, required her to do ten assignments, and allowed her to take the final on the date previously scheduled with her Home-Bound Instructor. I would have preferred that we followed the 504 regarding Home-Bound instruction for Math, kept the schedule for Heather as planned, and accepted the work as first arranged. The work that Heather was forced to do was accomplished with the Home-Bound Instructor and this gave her a passing grade of a 'C'. Again, I am grateful to this Home-Bound Instructor who rearranged her schedule at the last minute to help Heather achieve her goals.

Here's another incident where teachers were helpful. Since Heather did not come to school till late, she was not there for attendance. The school had paid a lot of money for a computerized attendance system that didn't operate properly. Though Heather had an excuse, she was marked absent everyday which is why I was so friendly with the Attendance Staff. I called almost every day to explain that Heather was not absent but was just starting late. One day Heather went to school to find that her locker had been emptied of all books and schoolwork. Can you say melt-down trigger? The school needed books so they ran an attendance report of students with high absences. Thinking these students had dropped out of school, they opened their lockers and took the books. Heather's school work had been thrown away and the books had already been given to other students. Some teachers copied portions of their books for Heather and gave her extra time and sometimes even excused work if she could pass her tests. The administrator who emptied out her locker admittedly had no training in Autism but I give him credit for apologizing to Heather. We were trying to show Heather even adults make mistakes; they apologize and you accept it. It was not done maliciously towards her.

Heather's story, good bad or indifferent, clearly tells what's wrong with education. If you ignore a child on the Autistic Spectrum simply because they pass using outdated educational testing, you guarantee to impact the health and well-being of that child in a negative manner. If you ignore the Sensory Processing Disorder aspect in a child and certainly one on the Autistic Spectrum, you guarantee to hurt them medically. How can any parent go into a current school environment where the school asks the parents to 'sign off' on supports that will be done that don't fully help that child or may hurt that child medically in the educating process?

I've spoken to many moms as I've branched out to support groups in four different states. They have the same problems at their schools to varying degrees. If the Autistic Spectrum Disorder characteristics increase in a certain environment and a child spends seven plus hours a day at school, it's a major part of their world. How can you not look at that educational environment and how can we not possibly have the most current training available to those in that system that are medically licensed to provide that? If Heather's story sounds negative, it was. Parenting a child on the Spectrum was scary, all-consuming, and hugely financially draining. It came with obstacles that were unnecessary like the fight with the Educational System and trying to secure local medical care. In my county, the local Disabilities Board doesn't recognize Asperger's Syndrome, High-Functioning Autism as a Developmental Disorder as does the medical community. I know a family who has two children with Asperger's. They moved here from the eastern part of the state because our small community was a better environment for their children. It was quieter than the city with a slower pace and a more conducive environment. They lost every support once they moved. The children's diagnoses didn't change simply because they lived in another town. The family moved back to regain supports.

We spent between $10,000. to $15,000 per year on supports. I know parents that spend $20,000-$25,000 per year. I was scared and anxious for my child. I couldn't control the emotion in my voice. I was grateful at times as I silently cheered that we'd gotten through one more day. When I talk to mothers that have children on the Spectrum, they understand this feeling. I was just having a discussion with one of those moms. She has a teenager on the Spectrum and we talked about how we never thought we'd see the other side of the struggle. We got our child back. There are good times with them and we have a semblance of normalcy in our family now. Like me, this mom became an advocate for other people.

I can't talk about Functioning Recovery without talking about a support group. There were none for Heather or for me. The closest supports were in Madison which was a forty-five minute drive away. We were also utilizing supports that weren't supported in Madison as of yet. It didn't seem that far but it was. We were struggling day to day in addition to therapies, socialization issues, melt-downs; etc. A forty-five minute drive was an eternity in addition to commuting to all the regular therapies. I had to recognize my limitations; I was exhausted. I was lucky though; I had Betsy and Honey, my friends in New Jersey. They listened, they were my sounding boards, I bounced ideas off of them, and I cried with them over struggles and obstacles. They listened to everything! There wasn't a situation where they didn't listen; they let me vent and helped to problem solve. They offered advice, recommendations, looked for and researched supports, and continue to support us today. Functioning Recovery for Heather would not have happened had we not been blessed to have them in our lives. Heather has commented that she needs a Honey and a Betsy of her own. They are my sisters and Heather's aunts by choice.

I feel compelled to make some comments about families. Everyone will have an opinion. I know whom in my family 'gets it' and who doesn't. Most likely, everyone has a family member who will disagree with what you're doing. Heather and I had a support group amongst our family. While visiting relatives when Heather was younger, we manipulated our schedule so she could have sensory time to reduce stress. I tried to shed some light on the situation before-hand but not everyone was receptive. I know they love Heather but when you don't live with Autism and SPD, it's hard to understand it. It took me awhile but I now accept each family member with 'where they are' with Heather.

It was especially difficult in the beginning of my research. I saw little clues in the children in my life, loved ones and friends' children. How did I not try to reach out and say something? How could I not help other parents? I know at times I tried to find the right words to express my concerns and sometimes parents were not receptive. It's disheartening, now, to hear that some of those children were diagnosed with an Autistic Spectrum or a Sensory Processing Disorder.

My intention with this book is to continue to network with other parents and families because it was networking that helped me to help Heather to achieve this Functioning Recovery. It was a step in the journey. When you network with other parents who are going through the same thing; you can support each other. That was my 'village'. That can be your 'village'. It will lead you to areas that you might not have dreamed. It gives you clues to how your child is. I listened to anyone who was going through a situation with their child because, maybe, part of their story would ring true and offer help for my child. I started hearing the same things about Bio-Medical Supports, about Sensory Processing, about developing a sensory diet that the child can self-access in various environments so they can adapt and function in those environments. This was my 'village' who aided in raising my child. Networking is an invaluable tool. *(For Tami's Networking Ideas, refer to Appendix F).*

I was given a beautiful pink bundle when Heather was born. I was excited to think of the events and milestones that would unfold with this little girl and thought of the special times we would share as Mother and Daughter. None of my dreams included this journey but with love and persistence, we made it to the other side. It took a long time to have that relationship with my daughter. Together, we now enjoy our Mother/Daughter time. I'm even grateful for the typical Mother/Daughter squabbles. It shows me how far we've journeyed and that we've finally **"come through the fog"**.

Conclusion

*Does the flame of a candle really extinguish if
it lights another candle?*

Anonymous

MY INTENTION FOR writing this book was to encourage networking
between families with children on the Autism Spectrum. As you have
read, our journey would not have unfolded to Functioning Recovery
had it not been for networking. Where would we be without the
sharing of information? My intent is to reach out to moms, dads,
primary caregivers, and/or teachers. If sharing my story helps them to
help their child or any child, it is a blessing.

Networking doesn't have to be in person; it is very easy to network on
the Internet. Any search engine yields a slew of networking sites. Even
Facebook opens doors for networking. Some of my favorite Facebook
pages include; My Autism Team, Sensory Planet, and Autism Moms.
There are running dialogues of questions and responses.

Networking led me to build relationships with people who have
become like family. Sometimes, a child and a parent only feel

comfortable discussing boyfriend relations to a certain point. When Heather was going through the boyfriend stage, I sought the support from a mom who also had a daughter on the Autism Spectrum though ten years younger than Heather. Just as that mom played the role of a Big Sister to guide and help Heather understand all of those relationship implications, I now see Heather acting as a Big Sister to this mom's daughter who's now sixteen years old.

My best times with Heather were in Occupational Therapy. We learned how to play together and I learned how to play in Heather's world. Through that play, she derived therapy and I was able to connect with her and see glimmers of the healthy woman within. I would never have seen this if I had not tried. I had to persevere.

I understood, early on, that something was not processing correctly for Heather. Later, it seemed as if every person had an opinion, some of which were very hurtful, about our situation. Whether it was comments about my child or my parenting skills, I knew in my heart what was best for Heather. Who could be a better advocate for her? Raising a child on the Spectrum opens your mind. It's a learning experience and a bonding experience for all involved. Learn together. Work together. Take it one day at a time! Take it an hour at a time or a minute at a time! It is a slow steady arduous process that can yield great results. Don't give up! Even Low-Functioning children on the Autism Spectrum can achieve a level of Functioning Recovery but you won't know their potential unless you try.

Though the journey to Functioning Recovery has unfolded, our story continues. Heather opted to work instead of continuing in school. She told me she felt she learned about how life really is by being in the work force and seeing how others did it. Heather is now happily living independently in a sensory-friendly home that she purchased on her own. She is working part time and is talking about going back to college. I know along the way we will continue to reach out and share our experiences.

> *I see people with Asperger's as a bright thread
> in the rich tapestry of life.*

> *– Dr. Tony Attwood*

Appendices

Appendix A
List of Tips

Here is Tip #1. Call your friends and ask if they know anyone who has a child on the Autism Spectrum. Get their name and number and call them. (Introduction)

Here is Tip #2. Get two folders each with separate pockets. Mark one for Education and the other for Medical. (Chapter Two)

Here is Tip #3: When securing medical coverage for your child with Autism, the diagnosis should come from a medical doctor, MD. If the diagnosis is made by a Mental Health Provider, PhD, your insurance will only cover mental health supports. With the MD diagnosis, it opens the door for coverage in OT, PT, and SLP. (Chapter Two)

Here is Tip #4: Any OT, PT, or SLP Professional working with your child, should be willing to have open discussions with you and allow you to observe their work or you should reconsider working with this Professional. (Chapter Three)

Here is Tip #5: Make sure you, as the parent, understand that as your child enters Middle School and/or High School their supports need to be increased. (Chapter Four)

Here is Tip #6: It is common for children with High-Functioning Autism to excel in Math and Music. (Chapter Four)

Here is Tip #7: If you have a child with Autism, you will need to create a Support Team available to your child within their school. (Chapter Four)

Here is Tip #8: Make decisions for your child even if they or the school don't like it or understand it. (Chapter Four)

Here is Tip #9: Do not be afraid to ask school personal, including Art, Music, Gym, cafeteria monitors, and/or library staff, what kind of training they've had in Autism. (Chapter Four)

Here is Tip #10: When working with a child with Autism, everyone should have the same goals and should be speaking the same language. (Chapter Four)

Here's Tip #11: Author, Brenda Smith-Myles, recommends having the school assign a one-on-one aide for your child to keep them on-task, organized, and focused. (Chapter Four)

Here is Tip #12: When planning activities with your child, beware of the potential for Hidden Curriculum. (Chapter Four)

Here's Tip #13: Anyone with special knowledge about your child can, by law, be included in your IEP. (Chapter Four)

Here's Tip #14: Wisconsin State Law allows you to tape-record your IEP meeting. (Chapter Four)

Here is Tip #15: The Parent Concern section of the IEP paperwork is the only place the parents get to have their say. (Chapter Four)

Here is Tip #16: Be specific about the written words in the IEP paperwork so you have a clear understanding of what the school's commitment is for services. On the modification page it should provide the specific information of the school's commitment, location, and duration of the support. Do not accept verbiage such as; " and/or" or " individual or classroom". (Chapter Four)

Here is Tip #17: As stated in the IEP Process Guidelines, a parent has the right to end the meeting at any time and reconvene at a later date. (Chapter Four)

Here is Tip #18: Prior to your child's eighteenth birthday, give the school a notarized letter allowing you to continue to have decision-making power for your child to avoid being excluded. (Chapter Five)

Here's Tip #19: A child with Autism is impacted medically if they are not receiving regular one-on-one OT support in school to build a sensory diet and it could affect their ability to achieve Functioning Recovery. (Chapter Five)

Here is Tip #20: Children with Autism don't understand lapsed time. A visual timer can be very helpful; they are designed so the child can see that time is elapsing. (Chapter Five)

Here is Tip #21: There are programs like <u>Floortime</u> and <u>RDI</u> (Relationship Development Intervention) that help and teach social skills. (Chapter Five)

Here is Tip #22: Allowing your child with Tactile Defensiveness to leave class five minutes before it ends, should allow your child to get through the school hallways before the entire student body is released. (Chapter Five)

Here is Tip #23: Children with Autism like structure, routine, and to follow rituals. (Chapter Five)

Here is Tip #24: Front-loading is an important support to reduce anxiety from a change in routine. It's a heads-up to the child with Autism that their regular routine is changing. The key is to allow adequate front-loading time; each child may require a different amount of time to process the change. For example, letting the child know right before the change may not allow their brains enough time to process. (Chapter Five)

Here is Tip #25: Many children with Autism have ocular motor issues. The eyes do not work together. It can affect their ability to read and move about their environment. Not all eye doctors are trained to evaluate for ocular motor skills. (Chapter Five)

Appendix B (from Chapter Three)
Resources with Websites

SENSORY PROCESSING DISORDER

[To find an occupational therapist certified in Sensory Integration go to: www.wpspublish.com/ In the search box put SI certified then select the state and enter.]

- SPD Network; www.spdnetwork.org/www.spdfoundation.org
  5420 S. Quebec St. Ste. 135
  Greenwood Village, CO 80111
  Phone: 303-794-1182 Fax: 303-322-5550

- Special Therapies; www.specialtherapies.com; Sue V. Kratz
  W238 N1690 Rockwood Dr., Ste. 500
  Waukesha, WI 53118
  Phone: 262-347-2222 Fax: 262-347-2251

- Sensational Kids: Help and Hope for Children with Sensory Processing
  www.sensationalkids.org; Dr. Lucy Jane Miller

- 1994 How Does Your Engine Run? Leader's Guide to the Alert Program for Self-Regulation; www.alertprogram.com; M. Williams and S. Shellenberger; Therapy Works, Inc.

7200 Montgomery NE, Ste. B9, Box 397
Albuquerque, NM 87109
Phone: 877-897-3478 Fax: 505-899-4071

- S.I. Focus; www.sifocus.com; The International Magazine
Dedicated to Improving Sensory Integration; SI Focus Magazine
PO Box 821404
Dallas, TX 75382
Phone: 214-341-9999

- Handwriting Without Tears; www.hwtears.com – handwriting
program by J. Olsen, OTR
806 Diamond Avenue, Suite 230
Gaithersburg, MD 20878
Phone: 303-263-2700 Fax: 301-263-2700

AUTISM

- Autism Society of America; www.autism-society.org
4340 East-West Hwy, Ste. 350
Bethesda, MD 20814
Phone: 301-657-0881 or 800-3autism [800-328-8476]

- Autism Research Institute; www.autism.com/ari; Bernard Rimland, PhD
4128 Adams Avenue
San Diego, CA 92116
Phone: 877-644-1184

- National Autism Association, www.nationalautismassociation.org
20 Alice Agnew Dr.
Antebora Falls, MA 02763
Phone: NAA-AUTISM [877-622-2884] Fax: 774-643-6331

BIO-MEDICAL SUPPORTS

- www.danprotocol.com; "Defeat Autism Now"

- www.elementalsliving.com

- www.generationrescue.com

CRANIOSACRAL THERAPY

www.upledger.com	The Upledger Institute; CranioSacral Therapy
www.SPDFoundation.net	SPD Foundation
www.SIFocus.net	SI Focus
www.sensoryPlanet.com	Sensory Planet
www.Senseabilities.com.au/	Catalogue for sensory supports and equipment
www.Wightslaw.com/	Special Education Law
www.AboutAutism.com	Autism
www.generationrescue.org	Vaccine information
www.aapcpublishing.net	Autism Asperger's publishing co.
www.autism-society.org	
www.autism.com	Autism Research Institute

Appendix C (from Chapter Four)
Definition of 504

A 504 plan refers to Section 504 of the Rehabilitation Act and the American with Disabilities Act. It specifies that no one with a disability can be excluded from participating in federally funded programs or activities, including elementary, secondary, or post-secondary school. Disability here refers to a physical or mental impairment which substantially limits one or more major life activities. A 504 plan spells out the modifications and accommodations that will be needed for these students to have an opportunity to perform at the same level as their peers. It may include the need for a wheelchair ramp, or a peanut-free environment, home-bound instruction, or technology for note taking. Unlike an IEP (Individualized Education Plan) which falls under the Individuals with Disabilities Education Act which is more concerned with actually providing educational services. Children eligible for an IEP require significant assistance and are more likely to work on their own level and at their own pace even in an inclusive classroom.

Appendix D (from Chapter Three)
Books

BY TEMPLE GRANDIN
<u>Emergence-Labeled Autistic</u>

<u>Developing Talents</u>

<u>Unwritten Rules of Social Relationships: Decoding Social Mysteries Through the Unique</u>

<u>Perspective of Autism</u>

<u>Different.. Not Less: Inspiring Stories of Achievement and Successful Employment from Adults with Autism, Asperger's, and ADHD.</u>

<u>Animals Make Us Human</u>

<u>The Way I See It: A Personal Look at Autism and Asperger's</u>

<u>Thinking in Pictures: My Life with Autism</u>

<u>Autism & Asperger's Syndrome</u>

By Brenda Smith-Myles
Asperger's and Adolescence: Practical Solutions for School Success

Asperger's Syndrome and Sensory Integration

By Anita C. Bundy, Shelly J. Lane & Elizabeth A. Murray
Sensory Integration Theory and Practice

By Dr. Lucy Jane Miller
Sensational Kids

By Carol Gray
The New Social Story Book

Writing Social Stories with Carol Gray

My Social Stories Book

The Original Social Stories Book

By Tony Attwood
The Complete Guide to Autism

Freaks, Geeks, and Asperger's

Asperger's Syndrome: A Guide for Parents and Professionals

By Carol Stock-Kranowitz
The Out of Sync Child

The Out of Sync Child Has Fun

Answers to Questions Teachers Ask About Sensory Integration

Resource for Books

Future Horizons, Inc.; www.futurehorizonsautism.com; Tony Attwood, PhD

721 West Abram Street
Arlington, TX 76013
Phone: 800-489-0727; Fax: 817-277-2270
Email: info@futurehorizons-autism.com

- Provides a list of national conferences and books on the autism spectrum and a bi-monthly magazine – Autism-Asperger's Digest

Appendix E (from Chapter Five)
Social Network Resources

Facebook

MyAutismTeam   My Autism Team-networking dialogue nation-wide

NSEL   National Special Education Law

Special Education Resources for Kids

SPDFoundation

SensoryPlanet

Sensory Connect

The Autism Society of America

Autism Support Network

Autism Mothers

National Autistic Society

Appendix F (from Chapter Six)
Tami's Networking Ideas & Additional Information

Applied Behavioral Analysis or ABA Therapy is a psychological approach where sessions involve one on one interaction between the behavior analysis and they participate. Developed by Dr. Lovaas, the approach is an intense system of reward-based training focused on particular skills. It is the oldest most researched therapy for Autism. Children with High-Functioning Autism like Asperger's usually are beyond this type of therapy.

Behavior Therapist is trained to help figure out what lies behind negative behaviors. They can be an asset as sensory detectives.

Social Skills Training – Help to teach social communication skills. Training helps build peer- based social interactions. Social Stories -Google - Carol Gray

Developmental Therapies – RDI (Relationship Developmental Intervention,) FloorTime or Son-Rise Developmental Therapy builds on the child's own interests and strengths to increase emotional, social and intellectual abilities.

Visual Based Therapies – PECS (Picture Exchange Communication, video modeling, video games, electronic communication devices build visual strength to build skill for communication.

Physical Therapist – to evaluate gross and fine motor skills. Evaluate for motor skill delays and low muscle tone. A Physical Therapist builds strength and coordination.

Resources

Wisconsin Department of Public Instruction
P.O Box 7841, Madison, WI 53707-7841
Ask for the Autism Consultant
Phone: 608-266-3928
Online refer to as DPI

Every state has a Department of Public Instruction*

DPI can address ; IDEA information, IEP procedures, IEP complaints, Mediation, Due Process, Open Enrollment for choice schooling, Homeschooling requirements and The Council on Exceptional Children. They also offer training and seminars open to parents.

Wisconsin Facets:
2714 N. Dr. Martin Luther King Dr. Milwaukee, WI 53212
Toll Free Phone: 877-374-4677 or 414-374-4645
WiFacets@WiFacets.org
http://wwww.WiFacets.org

Wisconsin Coalition for Advocacy
Phone: 608-267-0214

Every State offers some kind of advocacy services. Ask around. Go to PTA meetings, ask if there is a central education office call and ask them. Ask at the resource desk of your local library.

CranioSacral Therapy

www.Upledger.com

- Look under Find A Therapists, click Find A Practitioner
- The modality is CranioSacral Therapy
- Add your zip code for a therapist near you
- Broaden your search, also look under the zip codes of surrounding towns and cities.

A Therapeutic Touch by Tami LLC
www.IAHP.com/ATherapeuticTouch
Tami.CST1@Gmail.com

Networking Ideas

- Talk to people, expose yourself to more people that may know people going trying to raise a child with Autism. Ask questions!
- Use your Search Engine on line. Google it, it's as simple as that.
- Call the local medical facilities ask about supports groups for Autism, Sensory Processing Disorders, and/or Children with Disabilities.
- Call Psychologist offices
- Go to PTA meetings, Call the PTA at the State level.
- Ask about supports in surrounding areas.
- Ask at the resource desk of your local library. Look in surrounding communities or counties. Ask at those libraries.
- Ask around at your place of worship.
- Get on Facebook. There is a national and international world of networking supports on Facebook.

Appendix G
Timeline

Bolded = first occurrence or change

1987   **Heather's birth / sensitivities / tic**

1988   Sensitivities/ tic

1989   Sensitivities / tic / **2 year old shots / clumsiness / allergies**

1990   Sensitivities / tic / clumsiness / allergies

1991   **Pre-school** / sensitivities / tic **/ eye contact issues / non-interaction with other children / heavy sleeping / shut-downs**

1992   **Kindergarten** / sensitivities / **surgeries**

1993   **First Grade** / surgeries / tic / **moved to Wisconsin**

1994   **Second Grade** /sensitivities / tic /surgeries

1995   **Third Grade** / sensitivities / tic / surgeries / **diagnosis of ADHD**

1996	**Fourth Grade** / sensitivities / surgeries /2nd diagnosis of ADHD / **tic worsens / Dr. Mann's first recommendation for sensory supports in school.**
1997	**Fifth Grade** / surgeries / **seeking confined spaces** / tic worsens / **no R.E.M. sleep / Hepatitis B shots / Terra Nova tests**
1998	**Sixth Grade** / surgeries /seeking confined spaces / **weight loss / rashes /depression / School Psychologist recommends a 504 but no sensory supports.**
1999	**Seventh Grade** / surgeries / weight loss / **504 meetings / trouble with Math / Asperger's Diagnosis / Pediatrician B diagnosis of ADHD, short statute, mild anxiety-depression. Recommends medication, referral to mental health provider, endocrinologist, and "comprehensive plan of management." / Vol.29, No.2 Journal of Autism and Developmental Disorders publishes and documents why the ASSQ Autism Spectrum Screening Questionnaire, the evaluation tool used in the School District is not appropriate and no longer a current evaluation tool for High-Functioning Autism.**
2000	**Eighth Grade** / seeking confined spaces / weight loss / depression / 504 meetings / trouble with Math / **Special Ed. referrals / CranioSacral Therapy** / Terra Nova tests / **no Gym Class / 2nd diagnosis of Asperger's from UW-Health / Pediatrician A: letters to school district requesting modified school day and in-school supports.**
2001	**Freshman** / seeking confined spaces / **SPD / Independent OTR evaluation from Sue Kratz OTR, BCP / UW-Hospital evaluation** / trouble with Math /

CranioSacral Therapy / no Gym Class / **Independent Speech and Language evaluation for UW Health / Neuropsychologist evaluation from UW Health / Dr. Laird's report regarding** life-threatening **levels of stress hormones- recommendation for a modified school day** / Pediatrician A: letters to school district requesting modified school day and in-school supports on May 18, June 8, July 28, August 13, October 15, October 30, November 8, November 15, and November 20 / Stan and I remove authority allowing open communications between Heather's medical team and the school. Three medical professionals working with Heather refuse to deal directly with the school / School district refused to acknowledge information provided by doctors.

2002   **Sophomore** / SPD / adrenal stress hormones/ **updated evaluation and status from Sue Kratz OTR,BCP** / rouble with Math / CranioSacral Therapy / **modified school day** / no Gym Class

2003   **Junior** / SPD / adrenal stress hormones / Sue Kratz / trouble with Math / CranioSacral Therapy / modified school day / no Gym Class

2004   **Senior** / SPD / Sensory Processing / **updated evaluation and status from Sue Kratz OTR, BCP** / trouble with Math /CranioSacral Therapy / modified school day /

2005   **Heather has a part-time job**: **Pizza Hut** (phone orders, front counter)

2006   A part-time job: **The Armory Ticket Office**

2007	**Nail School** (No license but completed the course. Sensory issues prevented her from pursuing a career as a Nail Technician.)
2008	Nail School / **Blockbuster Video**
2009	Blockbuster Video (part time)
2010	Blockbuster Video (part time)
2011	Blockbuster Video (part time)
2012	**Ground Round Server (part time) / Heather purchases first home**

Contact Information

Tami A. Goldstein
A Therapeutic Touch by Tami, LLC

For questions or further information please feel free to contact Tami at:

www.iahp.com/ATherapeuticTouch

or

email: tami.cst1@gmail.com

CPSIA information can be obtained at www.ICGtesting.com
Printed in the USA
LVOW100657120313

323741LV00004B/5/P